THIS BOOK IS A GIFT FROM

THE FRIENDS OF THE WEST LAFAYETTE PUBLIC LIBRARY

2008

A BOOK IS A TREASURE TO OPEN AGAIN AND AGAIN

THE SECOND PLANE

The Second Plane

September 11: Terror and Boredom

MARTIN AMIS

ALFRED A. KNOPF
NEW YORK · TORONTO
2008

THIS IS A BORZOI BOOK

PUBLISHED BY ALFRED A. KNOPF

AND ALFRED A. KNOPF CANADA

Originally published in Great Britain by Jonathan Cape, a division of the Random House Group Ltd., London. Knopf, Borzoi Books, and the colophon are registered trademarks of Random House, Inc. Knopf Canada and colophon are trademarks.

Some of the pieces in this work originally appeared in the following: "On the Move with Tony Blair," "The Second Plane," "The Voice of the Lonely Crowd," and "The Wrong War" in *The Guardian;* " 'In the Palace of the End' " and " 'The Last Days of Muhammad Atta' " in *The New Yorker;* "Terror and Boredom: The Dependent Mind" in *The Observer;* "Iran and the Lord of Time" in The New York Times Syndicate; "An Islamist's Journey," "Bush in Yes-Man's-Land," "Conspiracy Theories, and *Takfir,*" "Demographics," "September 11," and "What Will Survive of Us," in *The Times.*

Library of Congress Cataloging-in-Publication Data

Amis, Martin.

The second plane : September 11 : terror and boredom / Martin Amis.

p. cm.

Includes index.

ISBN 978-1-4000-4454-2

1. United Airlines Flight 93 Hijacking Incident, 2001. 2. September 11 Terrorist Attacks, 2001. I. Title.

HV6432.7.A3836 2008

974.8'79044—dc22   2007040222

Library and Archives Canada Cataloguing in Publication

Amis, Martin, date.

The second plane : September 11 : terror and boredom / Martin Amis.

Includes index.

ISBN 978-0-676-97785-1

1. United Airlines Flight 93 Hijacking Incident, 2001. 2. September 11 Terrorist Attacks, 2001. I. Title.

HV6432.7.A58 2008   974.8'79044   C2007-907665-3

Manufactured in the United States of America

First North American Edition

To Delilah, Louis, Jacob, Fernanda, and Clio

Contents

Author's Note   ix

The Second Plane   3
The Voice of the Lonely Crowd   11
The Wrong War   21
"In the Palace of the End"   31
Terror and Boredom: The Dependent Mind   47
"The Last Days of Muhammad Atta"   93
Iran and the Lord of Time   123
What Will Survive of Us   129
Conspiracy Theories, and *Takfir*   137
Bush in Yes-Man's-Land   147
Demographics   153
On the Move with Tony Blair   159
An Islamist's Journey   187
September 11   193

Name Index   207

Author's Note

The fourteen pieces included here—two short stories and twelve essays and reviews—are reproduced in order of composition: an acknowledgment of the obvious truth that our understanding of September 11 is incremental and can never hope to be intact and entire. I have added to all of them (the Tony Blair travelogue has grown by 40 percent), and I have cut nothing, briefly tempting though it was, at times, to cover my tracks. For example, the first piece—published on September 18, 2001—has a slightly hallucinatory quality (it is fevered by shock and by rumor), and also indulges in what Paul Berman, the author of *Terror and Liberalism,* has called "rationalist naïveté"—a reflexive search for the morally intelligible, which always leads to the chimera of "moral equivalence." Similarly, the longest essay, "Terror and Boredom: The Dependent Mind," written in the midst of the Cartoons Affair and the Pope's inflammatory indiscretion, is rather heavy on "respect" for Islam. These misemphases are preserved. But I admit that I silently revised my remarks on Israel in the piece called "The Wrong War."

Terror and boredom are very old friends, as onetime residents of Russia (and other countries) will uneasily recall. The other face of the coin of Islamist terror is boredom—the nullity of the non-conversation we are having with the dependent mind. It is a mind with which we share no discourse. But if September 11 had to happen, then I am not at all sorry that it happened in my lifetime. That day and what followed from it: this is a narrative of misery and pain, and also of desperate fascination. Geopolitics may not be my natural subject, but masculinity is. And have we ever seen the male idea in such outrageous garb as the robes, combat fatigues, suits and ties, jeans, tracksuits, and medics' smocks of the Islamic radical? I was once asked: "Are you an Islamophobe?" And the answer is no. What I am is an Islamismophobe, or better say an anti-Islamist, because a phobia is an irrational fear, and it is not irrational to fear something that says it wants to kill you. The more general enemy, of course, is extremism. What has extremism ever done for *anyone*? Where are its gifts to humanity? Where are its works?

M.A., LONDON, AUGUST 2007

THE SECOND PLANE

The Second Plane

It was the advent of the second plane, sharking in low over the Statue of Liberty: that was the defining moment. Until then, America thought she was witnessing nothing more serious than the worst aviation disaster in history; now she had a sense of the fantastic vehemence ranged against her.

I have never seen a generically familiar object so transformed by *affect* ("emotion and desire as influencing behavior"). That second plane looked eagerly alive, and galvanized with malice, and wholly alien. For those thousands in the South Tower, the second plane meant the end of everything. For us, its glint was the worldflash of a coming future.

Terrorism is political communication by other means. The message of September 11 ran as follows: America, it is time you learned how implacably you are hated. United Airlines Flight 175 was an Intercontinental Ballistic Missile, launched in Afghanistan, and aimed at her innocence. That innocence, it was here being claimed, was a luxurious and anachronistic delusion.

A week after the attack, one is free to taste the bile of its atrocious ingenuity. It is already trite but stringently necessary to emphasize that such a *mise en scène* would have embarrassed a studio executive's storyboard or a thriller-writer's notebook ("What happened today was not credible" were the stunned and wooden words of Tom Clancy, the author of *The Sum of All Fears*). And yet in broad daylight and full consciousness that outline became established reality: a score or so of Stanley knives produced two million tons of rubble. Several lines of U.S. policy were bankrupted by the events of last Tuesday, among them national missile defense. Someone realized that the skies of America were already teeming with missiles, each of them primed and cocked.

The plan was to capture four airliners in the space of half an hour. All four would be bound for the west coast, to ensure maximum fuel load. The first would crash into the North Tower just as the working day hit full stride. Then a pause of fifteen minutes, to give the world time to gather round its TV sets. With that attention secured, the second plane would crash into the South Tower, and in that instant America's youth would turn into age.

If the architect of this destruction was Osama bin Laden, who is a qualified engineer, then he would certainly know something about the stress equations of the World Trade Center. He would also know something about the effects of ignited fuel: at 500°C (a third of the temperature actually attained), steel loses 90 percent of its strength. He must have anticipated that one or both of the towers would collapse. But no visionary cinematic genius could hope to re-create the majestic abjection of that double surrender, with the scale of the buildings conferring its own slow motion. It was well understood that an edifice so demonstrably comprised of concrete and steel would also become an unforgettable metaphor. This moment was the apotheosis of the postmodern era—the era of images and perceptions. Wind conditions were also favorable; within hours, Manhattan looked as though it had taken ten megatons.

Meanwhile, a third plane would crash into the Pentagon, and a fourth would crash into Camp David (the site of the first Arab-Israeli accord) or possibly into the White House (though definitely not into Air Force One: this rumor was designed to excuse Bush's meanderings on the day). The fourth plane crashed, upside down, not into a landmark but into the Pennsylvanian countryside, after what seems to have been heroic resistance from the passengers. The fate of the fourth plane would normally have been one of the stories of the year. But not this year. The fact that for the first few days one struggled to find more than a mention of it gives some idea of the size of the American defeat.

My wife's sister had just taken her children to school and was standing on the corner of Fifth Avenue and Eleventh Street at 8:58 a.m., on the eleventh day of the ninth month of 2001 (the duo-millennial anniversary of Christianity). For a moment she imagined herself to be on a runway at Kennedy Airport. She looked up to see the glistening underbelly of the 767, a matter of yards above her head. (Another witness described plane number one as "driving" down Fifth Avenue at 400 mph.) There is a modest arch that fronts Washington Square Park; American Airlines Flight 11 from Boston to Los Angeles was flying so low that it had to climb to clear it.

We have all watched airplanes approach, or seem to approach, a large building. We tense ourselves as the supposed impact nears, even though we are sure that this is a parallax illusion and that the plane will cruise grandly on. My sister-in-law was right behind Flight 11. She urged it to swerve, to turn into the plentiful blue sky. But the plane did not turn. That afternoon her children would be bringing refreshments to the block-long queue waiting to give blood at St. Vincent's.

Now the second aircraft, and the terror revealed—the terror doubled, or squared. We speak of "plane rage," but it was the plane itself that was in frenzy, one felt, as it gunned and steadied and then smeared itself into the South Tower. Even the flames and smoke were opulently evil, with their vampiric reds and blacks. Murder-suicide from without was now duplicated within to provide what was perhaps the day's most desolating spectacle. They flailed and kicked as they came down. As if you could fend off that abysmal drop. You too would flail and kick. You could no more help yourself than you could stop your teeth from chattering at a certain intensity of cold. It is a reflex. It is what human beings do when they fall.

The Pentagon is a symbol, and the WTC is, or was, a symbol, and an American passenger jet is also a symbol of indigenous mobility and zest, and of the galaxy of glittering destinations. The bringers of Tuesday's terror were morally "barbaric," inexpiably so, but they brought a demented sophistication to their work. They took these great American artifacts and pestled them together. Nor is it at all helpful to describe the attacks as "cowardly." Terror always has its roots in hysteria and psychotic insecurity; still, we should know our enemy. The firefighters were not afraid to die for an idea. But the suicide killers belong in a different psychic category, and their battle effectiveness has, on our side, no equivalent. Clearly, they have contempt for life. Equally clearly, they have contempt for death.

Their aim was to torture tens of thousands, and to terrify hundreds of millions. In this they have succeeded. The temperature of planetary fear has been lifted toward the feverish; "the world hum," in Don DeLillo's phrase, is now as audible as tinnitus. And yet the most durable legacy has to do with the more distant future, and the disappearance of an illusion about our loved ones, particularly our children. American parents will feel this most acutely, but we will also feel it. The illusion is this. Mothers and fathers need to feel that they can protect their children. They can't, of course, and never could, but they need to feel that they can. What once seemed more or less impossible, their protection, now seems obviously and palpably inconceivable. So from now on we will have to get by without that need to feel.

Last Tuesday's date may not prove epochal; and it should be the immediate task of the present Administration to prevent it from becoming so. Bear in mind: the attack could have been infinitely worse. On September 11 experts from the Centers for Disease Control "rushed" to the scene to test its atmosphere for biological and chemical weapons. They knew that these were a possibility; and they will remain a possibility. There is also the integrally insoluble hazard of America's inactive nuclear power stations (no nuclear power station has ever been dismantled, anywhere). Equivalent assaults on such targets could reduce enormous tracts of the country to plutonium graveyards for tens of thousands of years. Then there is the near-inevitable threat of terrorist nuclear weapons—directed, perhaps, at nuclear power stations. One of the conceptual tasks to which Bush and his advisers will not be equal is that the Tuesday Terror, for all its studious viciousness, was a mere adumbration. We are still in the first circle.

It will also be horribly difficult and painful for Americans to absorb the fact that they are hated, and hated intelligibly. How many of them know, for example, that their government has destroyed at least 5 percent of the Iraqi population? How many of them then transfer that figure to America (and come up with fourteen million)? Various national characteristics—self-reliance, a fiercer patriotism than any in Western Europe, an assiduous geographical incuriosity—have created a deficit of empathy for the sufferings of people far away. Most crucially, and again most painfully, being right and being good support the American self to an almost tautologous degree: Americans are good and right by virtue of being American. Saul Bellow's word for this habit is "angelization." On the U.S.-led side, then, we need not only a revolution in consciousness but an adaptation of national character: the work, perhaps, of a generation.

And on the other side? Weirdly, the world suddenly feels bipolar. All over again the West confronts an irrationalist, agonistic, theocratic/ideocratic system which is essentially and unappeasably opposed to its existence. The old enemy was a superpower; the new enemy isn't even a state. In the end, the U.S.S.R. was broken by its own contradictions and abnormalities, forced to realize, in Martin Malia's words, that "there is no such thing as socialism, and the Soviet Union built it." Then, too, socialism was a modernist, indeed a futurist, experiment, whereas militant fundamentalism is convulsed in a late-medieval phase of its evolution. We would have to sit through a Renaissance and a Reformation, and then await an Enlightenment. And we're not going to do that.

What *are* we going to do? Violence must come; America must have catharsis. We would hope that the response will be, above all, non-escalatory. It should also mirror the original attack in that it should have the capacity to astonish. A utopian example: the crippled and benighted people of Afghanistan, hunkering down for a winter of famine, should not be bombarded with cruise missiles; they should be bombarded with consignments of food, firmly marked LEND-LEASE USA. More realistically, unless Pakistan can actually deliver bin Laden, the American retaliation is almost sure to become elephantine. Then terror from above will replenish the source of all terror from below: unhealed wounds. This is the familiar cycle so well caught by the matter, and the title, of V. S. Naipaul's story "Tell Me Who to Kill."

Our best destiny, as planetary cohabitants, is the development of what has been called "species consciousness," something over and above nationalisms, blocs, religions, ethnicities. During this week of incredulous misery, I have been trying to apply such a consciousness, and such a sensibility. Thinking of the victims, the perpetrators, and the near future, I felt species grief, then species shame, then species fear.

SEPTEMBER 18, 2001. *The Guardian*

The Voice of the Lonely Crowd

> Were I (who to my cost already am
> One of those strange prodigious Creatures, Man)
> A Spirit free, to choose for my own share,
> What Case of Flesh, and Blood, I pleas'd to weare,
> I'd be a Dog, a Monkey, or a Bear
> Or any thing but that vain Animal
> Who is so proud of being rational.

These bitterly charged lines, from Lord Rochester's "Satyr Against Mankind," were written in 1675. They now seem somewhat premature, do they not? The age of reason, individuality, and empiricism was on its way; and Rochester was suspicious of the new reality. His worries were needless. On any longer view, man is only fitfully committed to the rational—to thinking, seeing, learning, knowing. Believing is what he's really proud of.

After a couple of hours at their desks, on September 12, 2001, all the writers on earth were considering the course that Lenin menacingly urged on Maxim Gorky: a change of occupation. I remember thinking that I was like Josephine, the opera-singing mouse in the Kafka story: Sing? "She can't even squeak." A novel is politely known as a work of the imagination; and the imagination, that day, was of course fully commandeered, and to no purpose. Whenever that sense of heavy incredulity seems about to dissipate, I still find, an emergent detail will eagerly replenish it: the "pink mist" in the air, caused by the explosion of the falling bodies; the fact that the second plane, on impact, was traveling at nearly 600 mph, a speed that would bring it to the point of disintegration. What was it like to be a passenger on that plane? What was it like to see it coming toward you?

An unusual number of novelists chose to write some journalism about September 11—as many journalists more or less tolerantly noted. I can tell you what those novelists were doing: they were playing for time. The so-called work in progress had been reduced, overnight, to a blue streak of autistic babble. But then, too, a feeling of gangrenous futility had infected the whole corpus. That page headed "By the same author"—which, in the past, was smugly consulted as a staccato biography—could now be dismissed with a sigh and a shake of the head. My own page, as an additional belittlement, ended with a book called *The War Against Cliché*. I thought: actually we can live with "bitter cold" and "searing heat" and the rest of them. We can live with cliché. What we have to do now, more testingly, is live with war.

Imaginative writing is understood to be slightly mysterious. In fact it is very mysterious. A great deal of the work gets done beneath the threshold of consciousness, and without the intercession of reason. When the novelists went into newsprint about September 11, there was a murmur to the effect that they were now being obliged to snap out of their solipsistic daydreams: to attend, as best they could, to the facts of life. For politics—once defined as "what's going on"—suddenly filled the sky. True, novelists don't normally write about what's going on; they write about what's not going on. Yet the worlds so created aspire to pattern and shape and moral point. A novel is a rational undertaking; it is reason at play, perhaps, but it is still reason.

September 11 was a day of de-Enlightenment. Politics stood revealed as a veritable Walpurgis night of the irrational. And such old, old stuff. The conflicts we now face or fear involve opposed geographical arenas, but also opposed centuries or even millennia. It is a landscape of ferocious anachronisms: nuclear jihad on the Indian subcontinent; the medieval agonism of Islam; the Bronze Age blunderings of the Middle East.

We recall that Ronald Reagan habitually anathematized the Soviet Union as "godless" (meaning, presumably, that its government was secular). This epithet could hardly be unleashed on Osama bin Laden. So Bush, who is religious, and Blair, who is religious, offered the patent falsehood that the war on terrorism was "not about religion." Iraq is godless too, but this fact is unlikely to be parlayed, just now, into another good reason for invading it.

The twentieth century, with its scores of millions of supernumerary dead, has been called the age of ideology. And the age of ideology, clearly, was a mere hiatus in the age of religion, which shows little sign of expiry. Since it is no longer permissible to disparage any single faith or creed, let us start disparaging all of them. To be clear: an ideology is a belief system with an inadequate basis in reality; a religion is a belief system with no basis in reality whatever. Religious belief is without reason and without dignity, and its record is near-universally dreadful. It is straightforward—and never mind, for now, about plagues and famines: if God existed, and if he cared for humankind, he would never have given us religion.

I was six or seven years old, and I was filling out a school registration form, and I came to the disquieting question, which seemed to visit me from a different world. I ran into the hall and shouted up the stairs, "Mum! What religion are we?" There was a long silence, then: "Uh . . . Church of England!" Yes, thank God for the Church of England: it didn't commit you to anything at all. In truth, though, "Church of England" was a mortal lie. We weren't even that.

Still, I felt an unwelcome distance from the families of my churchgoing friends (this was South Wales, in the 1950s). And I also developed a passion for my religious-knowledge mistress. It was an obscure passion: she was very nice, but she looked like an average witch in the picture-books I was then growing out of, complete with moles, warts, and facial hair of striking luxuriance. I didn't go to church but I did go to chapel (a soft-drinks party with the occasional parable); and I became a determined collector of Bibles. What you got, so it seemed, was a community and a language. My apostasy, at the age of nine, was vehement. Clearly, I didn't want the shared words, the shared identity. I forswore chapel; those

Bibles were scribbled on and otherwise desecrated, and two or three of them were taken into the back garden and quietly torched.

In my house, it would please me to claim, God just never came up. But that's not quite true. Later—we were now in Cambridge—my father spent a day with Yevgeny Yevtushenko, during which there was the following exchange. YY: "You atheist?" KA: "Well, yes, but it's more that I hate him." And in the home, when things went wrong, there was a certain amount of hating God, who was informally known as BHQ, or Bastards' Headquarters. At Cambridgeshire High School for Boys I gave a speech in which I rejected all faith as an affront to common sense. I was an atheist, and I was twelve: it seemed open-and-shut. I had not yet pondered Kant's rather lenient remark about the crooked timber of humanity, out of which nothing straight is ever built. Nor was I aware that the soul had legitimate needs.

Much more recently I reclassified myself as an agnostic, or left-agnostic or weak-agnostic; in any event, not quite an atheist. Because atheism, it turns out, isn't strictly rational either. The sketchiest acquaintance with cosmology will tell you that the universe is not, or is not yet, decipherable by human beings; we are ten or twelve Einsteins away from understanding it. Cosmology will also tell you that the universe is far more bizarre, prodigious, and chillingly grand than any doctrine, and that spiritual needs can be met by its contemplation. Belief is otiose; reality is sufficiently awesome as it stands. Indeed, our isolation in its cold immensity seems to demand a humanistic counterweight—an assertion of human pride. One contemporary manifestation of this need can be seen in our intensified reverence for the planet (James Lovelock's Gaia and other benign animisms). A strategy with a rather longer history centers on an intensified reverence for art—or, in Matthew Arnold's formula, for "the best which has been thought and said."

Literature—the aggregate of written works—has always been the most persistent candidate for cultification, partly because it nonchalantly includes the Bible and all other holy texts. It also has an advantage over conventional faiths in that there is, after all, something tangible to venerate— something boundless, beautiful, and divinely bright. But of course there is an excellent reason why the unacknowledged legislators of mankind are going to remain just that: unacknowledged and unfollowed. Literature forms a single body of thought, yet its voices are intransigently and unenlargeably individual. And the voice of religion, to reposition a phrase often used by that great critic, the Reverend Northrop Frye, is "the voice of the lonely crowd." It is a monologue that seeks the validation of a chorus.

In my lifetime there have been two attempts to ideologize and communalize literature. The first was the one undertaken by that grizzled relict, F. R. Leavis. Arnold wanted literature to occupy the spaces opened up by the weakening of faith and the unmoorings of the Industrial Revolution. At the outset (in the 1930s), Leavis called for the formation of an academic elite to oppose the vulgarisms of mass communication. His ideas were later systematized as follows: literature lives on only if there is someone around to evaluate it; the judgments the literary critic is concerned with (and this is the big leap) are judgments of life; so every judgment is an act of "moral responsibility" in the essential continuum. To put it another way, no good person likes the literature disliked by Dr. Leavis. It may be objected that literary value judgments are partly the products of emotion, and can never be arrived at by rational means alone (I. A. Richards and William Empson wasted years of their lives trying to systematize the separation of the excellent from the less excellent). But we do see that such an approach—the claim to central moral responsibility— wonderfully magnifies the national role of the English Literature don.

The Leavisite canon, never extensive, was fiercely defended and regularly purged. When I was at university you could always identify the Leavisites by the sorry dilapidation of their bookshelves. Conrad, James, George Eliot, some Austen, one Dickens (*Hard Times*), Yeats, T. S. Eliot, Hopkins, and a couple of vanished mediocrities like L. H. Myers and Ronald Bottrall. Left to itself, Leavisism might have ended up with a single text; and that sacred book would have been the collected works of an obvious sociopath—D. H. Lawrence. It had all gone wrong: they were supposed to be judging literature, but literature was judging them, and raucously exposing their provinciality and humorlessness. When Leavis died, in 1978, his clerisy collapsed in a Jonestown of *odium theologicum*. It left nothing behind it.

Leavisism was top-down, owing all its sway to the scrawny charisma of its prophet. The current ideology, known to us by the wearying clunk of its initials, is bottom-up, working through the mass and not away from it. There is a vague feeling that PC, having made its gains in the restriction of the sayable, is now in modest retreat. And it is true that the expansionist phase, with its denunciations, its invigilations, its organized execrations, seems to have run its course. On the other hand, PC now occupies the preferred territory of all ideologies: it is among schoolchildren. The language and literature papers in our national exams are becoming implicit invitations to ideological conformity; and everyone knows that there are few marks to be had for bucking the earnest line on, say, Maya Angelou. The weaker pupils will take the false comfort of belonging to a consensus; the stronger will simply receive early training in the practice of hypocritical piety.

We recognize this mental atmosphere, and its name is anti-intellectualism. Noticeable, too, is the re-emergence of sentiment as the prince of the critical utensils. Commentators respond, not to the novel, but to its personnel, whom they want to "care about," in whom they want to "believe." Such remarks as "I didn't like the characters" are now thought capable of settling the hash of a work of fiction. This critical approach will eventually elicit what it fully deserves—a literature of ingratiation. And we will then have reached the destiny that Alexis de Tocqueville predicted for American democracy: a flabby stupor of mutual reassurance. The simultaneous consolidation of "dumbing down" is not an accident. PC is low, low church, like the Church of England; it is the lowest common denomination.

And so we return to the writer's study, and mid-September 2001. The television, when you dared turn it on, showed Americans queueing for anthrax hosedowns, or the writhing mustaches of Pakistan, prophesying civil war and other unknowable sequelae. I remember the bad-dream feeling, and the dismaying inability to look with any pleasure at my children. Outside, the tinny city seemed to admit that its strategy of reason had been exploded. Even the plodding logic of the traffic lights looked obsolete. Why drive on the left? Why drive on the right?

The champions of militant Islam are, of course, misogynists, woman-haters; they are also misologists—haters of reason. Their armed doctrine is little more than a chaotic penal code underscored by impotent dreams of genocide. And, like all religions, it is a massive agglutination of stock response, of clichés, of inherited and unexamined formulations. This is the thrust of one of the greatest novels ever written, *Ulysses,* in which Joyce identifies Roman Catholicism, and anti-Semitism, as fossilizations of dead prose and dead thought.

After September 11, then, writers faced quantitative change, but not qualitative change. In the following days and weeks, the voices coming from their rooms were very quiet; still, they were individual voices, and playfully rational, all espousing the ideology of *no* ideology. They stood in eternal opposition to the voice of the lonely crowd, which, with its yearning for both power and effacement, is the most desolate sound you will ever hear. "Desolate," as it happens, provides the dictionary with one of its most elaborate poeticisms. "Desolate: giving an impression of bleak and dismal emptiness . . . utterly wretched . . . from L. *desolat-, desolare* 'abandon,' from *de-* 'thoroughly' + *solus* 'alone.'"

JUNE 2002. *The Guardian*

The Wrong War

We accept that there are legitimate casus belli: acts or situations "provoking or justifying" a recourse to arms. The present debate feels off-center, and faintly unreal, because the U.S. and the U.K. are going to war for a new set of reasons (partly undisclosed) while continuing to adduce the old set of reasons (reasons which in this case do not cohere). The new casus belli are a response to the accurate realization that we have entered a distinct phase in history. The coming assault on Iraq may perhaps be the Last War of the Ottoman Succession; it will certainly be the First War of the Age of Proliferation—the proliferation of weapons of mass destruction (WMDs). The new casus belli are also shaped by September 11.

September 11 has given to us a planet we barely recognize. In a sense it revealed what was already there, largely unremarked, since the collapse of the Soviet Union: the unprecedented preponderance of a single power. It also revealed the long-established but increasingly dynamic loathing of the West in the Islamic nations, a loathing much exacerbated by

America's relationship with their chief source of humiliation, Israel; this is a relationship that many non-Muslims consider unnatural, the present writer included (but for rather different reasons). In addition, like all "acts of terrorism"—easily and unsubjectively defined as organized violence that targets civilians—September 11 was an attack on morality: we felt a general deficit. Who, on September 10, was expecting by Christmastime to be reading unscandalized editorials in the *Herald Tribune* about the pros and cons of using torture on "enemy combatants"? Who expected Britain to renounce the doctrine of nuclear no-first-use? Terrorism undermines morality. Then, too, it undermines reason.

Osama bin Laden is an identifiable human type, but on an unidentifiable scale. He is an enormous stirrer—a titanic mixer. Look how he's shaken us up, both in the heart and in the head. One could say, countervailingly, that on September 11 America was visited by something very alien and unbelievably radical. A completely new kind of enemy, one for whom death is not death—and for whom life is not life, either, but illusion, a staging-post, merely "the thing which is called World." And, no, you wouldn't expect such a massive geohistorical jolt, which will reverberate for centuries, to be frictionlessly absorbed. But the suspicion remains that America is not behaving rationally—that America is behaving like someone still in shock.

The notion of the "axis of evil" has an interesting provenance. In early drafts of the President's State of the Union speech the "axis of evil" was the "axis of hatred," "axis" having been settled on for its associations with the enemy in the Second World War. The "axis of hatred" at this point consisted of only two countries, Iran and Iraq, whereas of course the original axis consisted of three (Germany, Italy, Japan). It was additionally realized that Iran and Iraq, while not both Arab, were both Muslim. So they brought in North Korea.

We may notice, in this *embarras* of the inapposite, that the Axis was an alliance, whereas Iran and Iraq are blood-bespattered enemies, and the zombie nation of North Korea is, in truth, so mortally ashamed of itself that it can hardly bear to show its face, and is not a part of anything. Still, "axis of hatred" it was going to be, until mature consideration turned the tide toward "axis of evil." "Axis of evil" echoed Reagan's "evil empire." It was more alliterative. It was also, according to President Bush, "more theological."

This is a vital question. Why, in our current delirium of faith and fear, would Bush want things to become more theological rather than less theological? The answer is clear enough, in human terms: to put it crudely, it makes him feel easier about being intellectually null. He wants geopolitics to be less about the intellect, and more about gut instincts and beliefs—because he knows he's got them. One thinks here of Bob Woodward's anecdote. Asked by Woodward about North Korea, Bush jerked forward saying, "I loathe Kim Jong-Il!" Bush went on to explain that the loathing sprang from his instincts, and added, apparently in surprised gratification, that it might be to do with his religion. Whatever else happens, we can infallibly expect Bush to get more religious: more gut-instinct, more theological.

When the somnambulistic figure of Kim Jong-Il subsequently threw down his nuclear gauntlet, the "axis of evil" catchphrase or notion or policy seemed in ruins, because

North Korea turned out to be much nearer to acquiring the definitive WMDs, deliverable nuclear devices, than Iraq (and the same is true of Iran). So why single out Saddam? It was explained that the North Korean matter was a diplomatic inconvenience, while Iraq's non-disarmament remained a "crisis." The reason was strategic: even without WMDs, North Korea could inflict a million casualties on its southern neighbor by flattening Seoul. Iraq couldn't manage anything on this scale, so you could attack it. North Korea could, so you couldn't. The imponderables of the proliferation age were becoming ponderable. Once a nation has done the risky and nauseous work of acquisition, it becomes unattackable. A single untested nuclear weapon may be a liability. But five or six constitute a deterrent.

From this it crucially follows that we are going to war with Iraq because it *doesn't* have weapons of mass destruction. Or not many. The surest way by far of finding out what Iraq has is to attack it. Then at last we will have Saddam's full cooperation in our weapons inspection, because everything we know about him suggests that he will use them all. The Pentagon must be more or less convinced that Saddam's WMDs are under a certain critical number. Otherwise it couldn't attack him.

All U.S. presidents—and all U.S. presidential candidates—have to be religious or have to pretend to be religious. More specifically, they have to subscribe to "born-again" Christianity. Bush, with his semi-compulsory prayer-breakfasts and so on, isn't pretending to be religious: "the loving God behind all life and all of history"; "the Almighty's gift of freedom to the world." "My acceptance of Christ," Bush has said (this is code for the born-again experience of personal revelation), "—that's an integral part of my life." And of ours, too, in the New American Century.

One of the exhibits at the Umm al-Maarik Mosque in central Baghdad is a copy of the Koran written in Saddam Hussein's blood (he donated twenty-four liters over three years). Yet this is merely the most spectacular of Saddam's periodic sops to the mullahs. He is, in reality, a career-long secularist—indeed an "infidel," according to bin Laden. Although there is no Bible on Capitol Hill written in the blood of George Bush, we are obliged to accept the fact that Bush is more religious than Saddam: of the two presidents, he is, in this respect, the more psychologically primitive. We hear about the successful "Texanization" of the Republican Party. And doesn't Texas sometimes seem to resemble a country like Saudi Arabia, with its great heat, its oil wealth, its brimming houses of worship, and its weekly executions?

The present Administration's embrace of the religious right also leads, by a bizarre route, to the further strengthening of the tie with Israel. Unbelievably, born-again doctrine insists that Israel must be blindly supported, not because it is the only semi-democracy in that crescent, but because it is due to host the Second Coming. Armageddon is scheduled to take place near the hill of Megiddo (where, in recent months, an Israeli bus was suicide-bombed by another kind of believer). The Rapture, the Tribulation, the Binding of the Antichrist: it isn't altogether clear how much of this rubbish Bush swallows (though Reagan swallowed it whole). V. S. Naipaul has described the religious impulse as the inability "to contemplate man as man," responsible to himself and uncosseted by a higher power. We may consider this a weakness; Bush, dangerously, considers it a strength.

Even a cursory examination of Saddam's character suggests that he will never fully disarm, any more than he would choose to revisit his childhood and walk shoeless and half-naked through the streets of Tikrit. Saddam respects WMDs: they averted defeat in the war with Iran. He started as he meant to go on when, in 1991, he appointed his younger (and less feral) son, Qusay, to the chairmanship of the Concealment Operations Committee. The assault on Iraq is expected to cost America 0.5 percent of its GDP; Saddam's wars, and the subsequent sanctions, have cost Iraq about twenty years' worth of GDP, according to *The Economist*. Such are his priorities. It has been in Saddam's power to alleviate the immiseration of his people. Instead, he has settled into a pattern of paranoia, gangsterism, and chronic kleptomania.

It is important to remember that Saddam, despite his liking for medals and camouflage outfits (and for personally mismanaging his armies), was never a military man. He came up through the torture corps in the 1960s, establishing the Baath secret police, Jihaz Haneen (the "instrument of yearning"), and putting himself about in the Qasr al-Nihayah ("the Palace of the End"), perhaps the most feared destination in Iraq until its demolition, after an attempted coup by the chief inquisitor, Nadhim Kazzar, in 1973.

Saddam's hands-on years in the dungeons distinguish him from the other great dictators of the twentieth century, none of whom had much taste for "the wet stuff." The mores of his regime have been shaped by this taste for the wet stuff—by a fascinated negative intimacy with the human body, and a connoisseurship of human pain. One is struck, too, by how routinely Saddam's organs have used familial love as an additional instrument of torture. Here, in moral terms, we decisively enter the Palace of the End, as the interrogator applies himself to your mother or your three-year-old child.

I said earlier that America's war aims remain partly undisclosed. The frank answer to the question "why now?," for instance, would be the usual jumble, something like: a) to pre-empt Saddam's acquisition of more WMDs; b) in good time for the next election; and c) before the weather gets too hot. Without his war, Bush is an obvious one-term blowhard; and he listens to his political handler, Karl Rove, at least as keenly as he listens to Donald Rumsfeld. The supplementary motivation, hatched at the think-tank and prayer-breakfast level, is, I fear, visionary in tendency. It has been noticed that a great deal of the world's wealth is in the hands of a collection of corrupt, benighted, and above all defenseless regimes. The war, as they see it, will not be an oil-grab so much as a natural ramification of pure power: manifest destiny made manifest reality, for the good of all.

Tony Blair must have known that the war was inevitable more than a year ago, when Bush started talking, with vulgar levity, of "taking Saddam out." In the past, Blair has been consistently tough on the Iraq question, just as France has been consistently and venally lenient (as early as the mid-1970s Jacques Chirac was known as "Monsieur Iraq"). More generally, perhaps, he feels that British interests are better served by continuing to ride on the American elephant, even as it trumpets its emancipation from the influence of Europe;

and that the total isolation of Washington would only heat Bush's internal brew of insecurity and messianism.

There are two rules of war that have not yet been rescinded by the new world order. The first rule is that the belligerent nation must be fairly sure that its actions will make things better; the second rule is that the belligerent nation must be more or less certain that its actions won't make things worse. America could perhaps claim to be satisfying the first rule (while admitting that the improvement may be only local and short term). It cannot begin to satisfy the second.

We contemplate a kaleidoscope of terrible eventualities: a WMD attack on Israel, and a WMD response (conceivably nuclear); civil war in Iraq, and elsewhere, together with all manner of humanitarian disasters; fundamentalist revolutions in Egypt and Jordan; and, ineluctably, an additional generation of terror from militant Islam. Meanwhile, common sense calmly states that an expanded version of the present arrangement (inspectors, "smart" sanctions, full exposure to world opinion) is sufficient to contain and emasculate Saddam until pressure builds for a coup; and that the "war on terror," the peace in the war on terror, can only start with the cautious giving of face (a gesture which the hegemon alone can make), and, say, the dismantling of the illegal settlements in the territories occupied by Israel.

But the necessary momentum has already been achieved, full deployment has been achieved, and the first humanitarian disaster will of course be the war itself.

O people of Iraq . . . By God, I shall strip you like bark,
I shall truss you like a bundle of twigs, I shall beat you

like stray camels . . . By God, what I promise, I fulfill; what I purpose, I accomplish; what I measure, I cut off.

You could imagine Saddam Hussein muttering these words when he assumed the presidency in 1979. It is with weariness and shame that we hear them from our own leaders, in various encryptions—faithfully echoing al-Hadjadj, the newly arrived governor of Iraq, in the year 694. And what al-Hadjadj measured, he cut off.

MARCH 2003. *The Guardian*

"In the Palace of the End"

As one of the doubles of the son of the dictator, I am quite often to be found in the Palace of the End. Six days a week, to be precise: and twelve hours a day. Actual public impersonations of the successor (parades, investitures, going on television, and the like) are by now a thing of the past. But we have our standing duties. In the mornings I set about my work in the Interrogation Wing. Then, in the afternoons, following a glass of scented coffee with the other doubles, I make filmed love to — or have filmed sex with — a series of picked beauties in the Recreation Wing. The Palace of the End is built in the shape of a titanic eagle: the beaked head downturned, the scalloped pinions out-thrust . . . It was the brainchild of Old Nadir, who is very slowly dying of the injuries he sustained in the notorious "toilet bomb" assault at another of his palaces, in the south of our country. And now all power rests with his only son: Nadir the Next.

Until recently, at least, my work in the Interrogation Wing was not particularly onerous. I wasn't obliged to participate in the full course of the numerous procedures. *My* job was to "appear," with surreal suddenness, at the climax of this or that cross-questioning (which might have gone on for days or weeks); flanked by armed infantrymen, I would stamp into the cubicle, wearing camouflage fatigues and cripplingly heavy combat boots, and administer one backhand blow to the suspect's face. And that was all. But nowadays, for several reasons, I am expected, as are the other doubles, to apply myself more variedly. We have not exactly been reduced to the status of mere bucket-boys and poker-warmers—no; but in these tense times we must put ourselves about and show willing.

The interior of the Interrogation Wing used to be laid out in the traditional "cells and cellars" arrangement: dripping passageways, clanking iron doors, rooms within rooms ("the kennels"), and so on—with the howls and screeches of the suspects decently muffled or snatched or cut short. Now it's open-plan. One enters an anti-hospital, a vast factory of excruciation: there the strappado, here the bastinado; there the rack, here the wheel. The more communal atmosphere is meant "to discourage the others," and it's certainly true that, from the suspect's point of view, the induction into the Interrogation Wing is far worse than any death. Indeed, it was more or less universal practice for the prisoners to attempt instant suicide by the only means available—by the dental excision, that is to say, of their own tongues.

However understandable, this practice also entrained a paradox: the tongueless ones, their mouths moreover crammed with soiled gauze, could neither proclaim their innocence nor (by far the wiser course) trumpet their guilt. But in the end it made no difference. At a certain point—

perhaps months later—the suspect's head would give a lolling nod, and the interrogator would stroll to the old Xerox machine for the standard confession (which the suspect would then initial). After more torture preludial to death, 99 percent of those who enter the Interrogation Wing are eventually hanged; the remainder are sent home fatally envenomed, with a day or two to live—and, no doubt, a tale or two to tell. The tongueless ones cannot tell their tale, but they can sketch it, write it, mime it, while they live. Thus would they too play their part in shoring up respect for the essentially personal rule of Nadir the Next.

Anyway, these days the question of the tongueless ones is academic. There are no more tongueless ones. All suspects now have their teeth smashed and pulled in the anteroom of the Reception Hall, long before they are even fingerprinted by the registrars.

At twelve forty-five the doubles congregate in the doubles' commissary, which is situated in the main body of the building—in the golden eagle's muscular torso. At any given time there are thirty or forty doubles stationed at the Palace of the End (though there are scores of us in the capital, and dozens more in every major provincial town). Idling and milling around the doubles' commissary, we enjoy a glass of coffee, and a sliver of nougat, perhaps, while we ready ourselves for the work of the afternoon. First, the work of the morning. Then the work of the afternoon.

For a double, this interlude in the doubles' commissary

can be a slightly depersonalizing experience. We all measure six feet one, and we all weigh 257 pounds. We all have the same glistening black quiff, the same protuberant, blood-flecked brown eyes, the same slablike front teeth (with the same missing canine), the same patch over the same eye. We wear an eyepatch because Nadir wears an eyepatch; and Nadir wears an eyepatch because he was shot in the face, by a bodyguard, seventeen months ago. And here I touch on one of the more somber duties of a presidential double. All the injuries picked up by Nadir, during the course of the increasingly frequent and desperate attempts on his life, must naturally be duplicated in his surrogates. For the blast to the left eye, we were, in turn, strapped and clamped into position with an automatic pistol poised on a tripod at a distance of eighteen inches; many doubles were lost in the initial efforts (despite numerous experiments on an assortment of suspects), and many more were decommissioned, and quietly executed, when their wounds failed to heal in the proper way. Similarly, every double lacks a right kneecap, a left heel, a left shoulder blade, and the fourth and fifth fingers of his left hand. We have all spent time in wheelchairs, on crutches, in neck braces, in traction. We are additionally subject to periodic poisonings. More recently, we all had our hair scorched off (after a flame-thrower attack on the son of the dictator), and for a while a team of barbers and surgeons appeared every day to regulate the condition of our fuzz and blisters.

Entering the doubles' commissary is, as I say, a depersonalizing experience. It is to enter a hall of mirrors. Who is that man by the window with his back turned to the room? He slowly swivels. Again, yes: it is I . . . There's no little pleasure to be had, of course, in mingling with one's peers. But the conversation is always somewhat strained. It isn't just the presence of five or six full-time informers, posing as doubles—for we are all informers, and inform on one another as a matter of daily routine. No. It is the feeling (entirely unfounded) that Nadir himself is perhaps among us. Once in a while, as you pass the time of day and complain about the weather, you sense in your interlocutor a wavering heat in the eyes, and a heat from the body (and a hot smell, too: the smell of power) that seems to betray the proximity of the son of the dictator. At such moments, both speech and silence become inconceivable—alive, as we all are, to the well-attested sensitivity, and short temper, of Nadir the Next.

There is one double, and one double only, with whom I feel I can be more or less myself—Mekhlis. For a start, I can always tell it's him: like me, Mekhlis had a large facial mole removed (or, rather, relocated), and there is a circular blur on his cheek that matches the blur on mine. Today I edged up to Mekhlis in the conservatory bay that leads out to the gardens—the gardens, with their parrots and apes. I said,

"What was in that *sack?*"

"*What* sack?" he answered in the same gross baritone. Our trouble is that our tongues are too big: too big for our mouths. "Oh *that* sack," he said.

Earlier that morning I had spent an abnormally uncomfortable half-hour yelling at a suspect while a blood-steeped canvas mailbag jerked and jumped around the cubicle floor. The scream it emitted put one in mind of a boiling kettle.

"Yes," he said. "A severe measure. The sack contained

some starving animals plus the suspect's three-year-old daughter."

"So I imagined. But wasn't there something unusual about the animals?"

"Not in themselves. You know—'bats and cats and rats.' But the vet said they'd been overstarved. Too listless. So he gave them all a shot. Amphetamine. A very stubborn case."

"Why do they not instantly confess?" I said. "Why don't they sign with a flourish—on entry?"

We shook our heads and wiped our brows. Again, the mirror feeling: I am him and he is me.

"The untongueless ones—does nobody listen to them?"

"They may listen," he said, "but they don't believe. And they're innocent. In Old Nadir's day at least *some* of them were guilty. But this lot. It's hard to confess if you're innocent."

And the consciousness of innocence must be a very powerful thing, I thought. I said, "Then they don't understand. Guilt, innocence: this is not the way of the Next. Perhaps it would be better if we . . ."

But then a third double drew near, and Mekhlis fell to talking about the dust storms.

At 1:15 we filed out to the locker room, where, six days a week, we exchange our combat boots for pointed slippers and our camouflage fatigues for cream kimonos; the black beret is doffed in favor of the pomaded tarboosh with its crimson tassel.

Somehow the months pass.

.   .   .

On to the Recreation Wing, with its conditioned air, its piped music, its picked beauties. Until quite recently, Nadir was having us consort with women of the Jezebel type: demi-mondaines, belly dancers, oiled houris. And we were under the strictest instructions to use them roughly. All that's over. The policy change began when Nadir was shot in the leg, and became radical when he was shot in the face. No longer the snarling sodomizings, the raucous "squad bangs," and so on. Now we recline in luxurious apartments with our ladyfriends of the afternoon; we feed them peeled jargonelles drenched in choice liqueurs; I might softly declaim a few verses of the immortal poet, Narciso, as I reach for my lute. Then, at 2:50, you become aware of the activation of the camera, and you proceed.

Nowadays, a double's best possible result, in the Recreation Wing, is to bring about multiple orgasm. Any kind of orgasm at all is an inestimable prize; and a solid success rate is usually enough to protect a double from disfavor or disgrace or disaster. But multiple—and preferably continuous—orgasm is what we always feel we have to aim for, and it is not an entirely happy double who, sipping his cola with the other doubles at 7:35, has failed, that day, to achieve it.

At the time, it was widely thought that the reason for Nadir's change of course was baldly utilitarian. He had, by then, simply run out of odalisques and filles de nuit, and was now working his way through the general population: young nurses, young secretaries, young schoolteachers—nearly all of them young widows, needless to say. I do not subscribe to this theory (and am attempting to formulate my own). But the fact is that the double now confronts an altogether different kind of challenge in the Recreation Wing. On entry into its apartments, as I made the air hum with my switch, I used to encounter an ogreish wink and a lewd roll of the tongue. Now I encounter the isolated stare of the girl next door, and do so with a nosegay and a box of chocolates in my hands. Mekhlis claims he speaks for all the doubles when he says that he liked it much, much better in the old days. Well, he doesn't speak for me. The new pressures faced by a double push down into the very lining of a man, and involve mortal danger— not least from suicide. But I wouldn't go back. No, I wouldn't go back.

Your first objective, of course, is to still the trembling. Normally you would hope to get this out of the way over lunch: you calmly adumbrate what lies ahead, and list the penalties and perquisites attending failure or success. The young women are also very sharply warned that the lengthy and invasive verification process—which includes a poly-graph test and an injection of scopolamine—will expose all attempts at simulation: such an orgasm, as interpreted by the Next, is a mortal affront. This often makes them tremble all the more. In fact, some of them go on trembling well into the afternoon, despite the skilled foot-massage, the reciprocal ablutions, the application of many a telling unguent. Some of them never stop trembling, and the task, in these cases, is to find the deeper rhythm or logic of it, and so transform vibration into vibrancy. It is not the work of a moment.

Today, for example, I entertained a young anesthetist from the provincial capital. I toasted her with French champagne, I crooned love songs to the accompaniment of my theorbo, and recited certain stanzas in praise of her pulchritude, which was considerable and highly refined, despite the seraglio outfit and the ghoulish maquillage on which Nadir still invariably insists—and despite the cladding of hatred in her eyes. The young anesthetist's hands and voice slowly steadied. But when I romantically hoisted her into my arms and carried her to the klieg-lit cushions she felt like a bronze statue (one of the more modest statues of the Next, perhaps)—all suppleness and buoyancy lost, and the flesh as cold and adhesive as dry ice. Toward the end of the third hour of unpunctuated cunnilingus, I thought I might be starting to get somewhere; but in the end the young anesthetist was unable to respond. She will lose her internal passport and her right to medical assistance (and so will all her family). As for me, the non-satisfaction, the anticlimax, will go on my P-card. It will be noticed.

We used to have the ability, sometimes, to arouse them with our beauty—for we once were beautiful. But not now, in these tense times. Regrettably, during his various incapacitations, the Next has now gained some ninety-five pounds. And there are also the hideous "splatter wounds" to his chest and back, sustained in a dual RPG and IED assault while he was traveling underground by monorail. Then, too, there was the hit from the ATS—or anti-tank shell— he took in the ballroom of yet another palace; he was standing beneath the two-ton chandelier as it fell, and was pierced by stupendous quantities of inch-thick glass. No, we are not beautiful any longer. One vast lesion: that's what I am. When the doubles shower together—and there are barely twenty of us now — we look all red and raw, like a convocation of colossal penises.

The darkest moment of the day, I find (surprisingly, perhaps), is the change: the unlacing of the combat boots, the adoption of the pointed slippers. This is when I have to deal with my humanity, and answer the questions put to me by my wizened soul. We are not permitted to wash until eight in the evening; and as I slip the richly perfumed kimono over my head I can smell all the dread and fury of the Interrogation Wing. And then it is that I gird myself for the next craven honey-blonde, the next veal-pale brunette, the next resplendently contemptuous redhead. And all of them always trembling.

Obviously, an "anticlimax" is very far from being considered a success. But there is a whole other order of failure — a whole other universe of failure. We don't talk about it. Mekhlis doesn't talk about it. I don't talk about it. This explains the fact that the moment in the changing room is also, if you like, a confession: a confession of the male vulnerability and flaw . . . To err is human. Every double does it — on occasion. But we all know the point at which we can expect the lavish, the inwrought wrath of the potentate. And we all know why this second order of failure — so radical, so all-deciding — especially incenses Nadir the Next.

At nine o'clock we repair to our separate bungalows in the grounds. Fraternization among doubles used to be vigilantly discouraged (to thwart plotting), but now, in these days of laxity and dissolution, as the Next weakens, as we weaken, there is a more or less nightly bazaar of black-market aphro-disiacs in our compound, all kinds of potions and philters— every known pharmaceutical, as well as every known quackery. To step out into the capital is of course an impos-sibility; a double wouldn't last half a minute in the capital, or anywhere else. But here at night, with all these pots and packets and powders, so needfully assembled and dispersed, we can still get a sense of the forgotten static of the city.

I stand before the mirror. I am choking on my own tongue—it looks like the fin of a flayed shark—and must soon submit to my third lingual "carve-down." Is that my-self I see, or am I staring through a window at another dou-ble? . . . We break mirrors. Doubles are always breaking mirrors. The vital thing is to resist the impulse to do so with a butt of the forehead. Keep a hammer nearby. It's on the rest day that you notice it. Servants, workmen, going to and fro with mirrors, broken mirrors, fresh mirrors. And heaps of smashed glass like ponds of fire in the midday sun.

The months pass. And it can't be long now. For us, and for the Next—so ceaselessly are his bastions mined, his bunkers tripwired, his bolt-holes booby-trapped.

Some doubles say that there have been worse times to be a double. Years ago, before my arrival at the Palace of the End, the son of the dictator used to send the doubles out to give fiery speeches in city squares, to parade in open limousines, to march at the head of ticker-tape tattoos. All, of course, were briskly assassinated, thus somewhat alleviating, for a short time (or so he felt), the danger posed to the Next.

Other doubles say there have been *better* times to be a double: when, for instance (this is Mekhlis), the doubles were asked to uphold their mercilessness as they moved from one wing to the other. You make your "pact with pain," he says — and that's that; besides (he argues), rape is less boring, and much quicker, than the marathon "tongue work" expected of us now. I haven't forgotten those days, and the mental atmosphere was certainly very different. More high-strung, you might say. Even the coffee break was like a prison riot.

Enmeshed in an atrocity-producing situation, the human being, I have read, responds with one of two psychological strategies or mechanisms. The first is called "numbing." I remember numbing: it resembled submission to a drug of unwelcome and alien efficacy. The second strategy or mechanism, curiously, is called "doubling." That's what we all do now. There is the person of the morning, and then, following the period in the changing room, there is the person of the afternoon.

And we doubles *have* doubled. I think I can prove it. The laws of our country do not permit the execution of female virgins. Circumventing this stricture, by mass rape, used to be one of our privileges. But ever since Nadir was shot in the face, and the Recreation Wing was refurbished for romance, no double will have anything to do with the "squad bangs" on the scaffolds. We leave all that to the bucket-boys and poker-warmers and the other, humbler torturers of the Interrogation Wing.

The destiny of the failed double (one who repeatedly creeps in tears from the luxurious apartments with the rims of his pointed slippers held between finger and thumb) is probably worth mentioning. Such a double must watch all his clan submit to the antic horror of the confessionals, but the double himself is dispatched by lethal injection—put to sleep, like a toothless dog. No further harm or disfigurement is visited on his body.

This morning, as I was about to supervise the "de-gloving" of an elderly suspect, Mekhlis, in contravention of a major ground rule (doubles are never to be seen plurally in the Interrogation Wing), took me aside and passed on the rumor of the latest attempt on the life of the son of the dictator. I had just started work, and so there were several hours to get through before I limped into the doubles' commissary at 12:45.

There are only seven doubles now. Some have died from complications arising from their more recent injuries (notably the bazooka attack); some have taken their own lives. Many, after grimly monotonous failure, have attracted the special execration of the Next . . . Because, you see, Nadir is impotent. He has ever been impotent. All his grown life, helpless, as in a dream, surrounded by naked women he could do nothing with.

Where there is no settled truth, rumor stops feeling like rumor: briefly but palpably, it feels far more convincing than any mere *fact* . . . The doubles' commissary was of course an aviary of mobile phones, and for the first hour I just sat there, strafed by the usual tumult of calamity. A mortar blitz, a kiloton daisy-cutter, a thermobaric cruise missile. Semtex, botulism, acid shell, carcinogenic aflatoxin, particle beam, Agent Orange. After a while, and again as usual, the rumors became rather milder (Nadir had simply been bayonetted in the guts, poleaxed in the groin, harpooned in the head), and then milder still. Some cook, it seemed, had tried to serve him a rotten egg. Some kid, it seemed, had thrown a pebble at his armored pantechnicon. Then re-escalation—all the way back to certain death.

Which is what we prayed for, naturally. Certain death. That way we had a chance. We doubles are not like the doubles of Old Nadir. Because Nadir the Next is also Nadir the Last.

"Come," said Mekhlis.

And together we hobbled into the conservatory bay: the gardens, with their parrots and apes.

"I think we should prepare ourselves," he said, "for an injury of the middle range. An arm."

"A foot. Maybe an ear."

"Maybe the other eye."

I said, "The other eye? What would that mean for our work of the afternoon? We could still do it, I suppose. It would be harder. But we could still do it."

"Yes," he said. "But think. Why would he want us to?"

His phone gave its gurgle. He looked at the screen and said heavily, "My cousin's friend at Special Forces." And then: "Yes. This is Double Mekhlis."

I'm sitting on the bench in the changing room, under the marquee of my cream kimono. By my side, the tasseled tarboosh; at my feet, the pointed slippers. I am wondering, as I always do at this time of day, why the body's genius for pain so easily outsoars its fitful talent for pleasure; wondering why the pretty trillings of the bedroom are so easily silenced by the impossible vociferation of the Interrogation Wing; and wondering why the spasms and archings of orgasm are so easily rendered inert and insensible by the climactic epilepsy of torture. You don't need to dim the lights for torture, or play soft music. People will respond. You don't need to get them in the mood. Everyone's always in the mood. And consider how pain can be made to ramify and proliferate. Where is the role, in the realm of pleasure, for the three-year-old daughter, for the mailsack, the rodent, the amphetamine?

It is all over now, anyway. The fate of Nadir the Next? From a double's point of view, it was pretty well the worst possible outcome. In his quest for peace and quiet he had taken to his submarine—for a week-long wallow on the floor of the Red Sea. That morning, after breakfast, he went to the bathroom with a newspaper under his arm . . . The dreaded "toilet bomb." The toilet bomb—now doubly legendary. He will join his father in the spaceship of intensive care, his center of gravity replaced by a raw hollow. And we will go the way of the doubles of Old Nadir. The fetish of verisimilitude will draw each of us to the sandbagged cell and its rigged white bowl, with the stool-sensitive limpet mine tucked into the U-bend, and the surgical team standing by.

This afternoon in the Palace of the End I shall strive, as Nadir's proxy or prosthesis, to be ever more tremulously tender. I think I understand this gravitation of the Next's: the tendency to the tender, in the Recreation Wing. I am well placed to empathize with him, after all—and I feel something like a hard vacuum in the side of our heads where our eye used to be. But I am not the Next. I am only his double. And my share of it reads like this. When you have been hurt yourself, there awakens a part of you that doesn't want to hurt anyone. When you love something as intimately fragile as your own body, you don't want to hurt anyone. That's what I'm saying to myself, now, in the changing room. Please let me not have to hurt anyone.

MARCH 2004. *The New Yorker*

Terror and Boredom:
The Dependent Mind

It was mid-October 2001, and night was closing in on the border city of Peshawar, in Pakistan, as my friend—a reporter and political man of letters—approached a market stall and began to haggle over a batch of T-shirts bearing the likeness of Osama bin Laden. It is forbidden, in Sunni Islam, to depict the human form, lest it lead to idolatry; but here was Osama's lordly and unintelligent visage, on display and on sale right outside the mosque. That mosque now emptied, after evening prayers, and my friend was very suddenly and very thoroughly surrounded by a shoving, jabbing, jeering brotherhood: the young men of Peshawar.

At this time of day, their equivalents, in the great conurbations of Europe and America, could expect to ease their not very sharp frustrations by downing a lot of alcohol, by eating large meals with no dietary restrictions, by racing around to one another's apartments in powerful and expensive machines, by downing yet more alcohol as well as additional stimulants and relaxants, by jumping up and down for several hours on strobe-lashed dance floors, and (in a fair number of cases) by having galvanic sex with near-perfect strangers. These diversions were not available to the young men of Peshawar.

More proximately, just over the frontier, the West was in the early stages of invading Afghanistan and slaughtering Pakistan's pious clients and brainchildren and brother Pathans, the Taliban, and flattening the Hindu Kush with its power and its wrath. More proximately still, the ears of these young men were still fizzing with the battle cries of molten mullahs, and their eyes were smarting anew to the chalk-thick smoke from the hundreds of thousands of wood fires—fires kindled by the multitudes of exiles and refugees from Afghanistan camped out all around the city. There was perhaps a consciousness, too, that the Islamic Republic of Pakistan, over the past month, had reversed years of policy and decided to sacrifice the lives of its Muslim clients and brainchildren and brother Pathans, over the border, in return for American cash. So when the crowd scowled out its question, the answer needed to be a good one.

"Why you want these? You like Osama?"

I can almost hear the tone of the reply I would have given—reedy, wavering, wholly defeatist. As for the substance, it would have been the reply of the cornered trimmer, and intended, really, just to give myself time to seek the fetal position and fold my hands over my face. Something like: "Well, I *quite* like him, but I think he rather overdid it in New York." No, that would not have served. What was needed was boldness and brilliance. The exchange continued:

"You like Osama?"

"Of course. He is my brother."

"He is your *brother*?"
"All men are my brothers."

All men are my brothers. I would have liked to have said it then, and I would like to say it now: all men are my brothers. But all men are not my brothers. Why? Because all women are my sisters. And the brother who denies the rights of his sister: that brother is not my brother. At the very best, he is my half-brother—by definition. Osama is not my brother.

Religion is sensitive ground, as well it might be. Here we walk on eggshells. Because religion is itself an eggshell. Today, in the West, there are no good excuses for religious belief—unless we think that ignorance, reaction, and sentimentality are good excuses. This is of course not so in the East, where, we acknowledge, almost every living citizen in many huge and populous countries is intimately defined by religious belief. The excuses, here, are very persuasive; and we duly accept that "faith"—recently and almost endearingly defined as "the desire for the approval of supernatural beings"—is a world-historical force and a world-historical actor. All religions, unsurprisingly, have their terrorists: Christian, Jewish, Hindu, even Buddhist. But we are not hearing from those religions. We are hearing from Islam.

Let us make the position clear. We can begin by saying, not only that we respect Muhammad, but that no serious person could fail to respect Muhammad—a unique and luminous historical being. He remains a titanic figure, and, for Muslims, all-answering: a revolutionary, a warrior, and a sovereign, a Christ *and* a Caesar, "with a Koran in one hand," as

Bagehot imagined him, "and a sword in the other." Judged by the continuities he was able to set in motion, Muhammad has strong claims to being the most extraordinary man who ever lived. And always a man, as he always maintained, and not a god. Naturally we respect Muhammad. But we do not respect Muhammad Atta.

Until recently it was being said that what we are confronted with, here, is "a civil war" within Islam. That's what all this was supposed to be: not a clash of civilizations or anything like that, but a civil war within Islam. Well, the civil war appears to be over. And Islamism won it. The loser, moderate Islam, is always deceptively well represented on the level of the op-ed page and the public debate; elsewhere, it is supine and inaudible. We are not hearing from moderate Islam. Whereas Islamism, as a mover and shaper of world events, is pretty well all there is.

So, to repeat, we respect Islam—the donor of countless benefits to mankind, and the possessor of a thrilling history. But Islamism? No, we can hardly be asked to respect a creedal wave that calls for our own elimination. More, we regard the Great Leap Backward as a tragic development in Islam's story, and now in ours. Naturally we respect Islam. But we do not respect Islamism, just as we respect Muhammad and do not respect Muhammad Atta.

I will soon come to Donald Rumsfeld, the architect and guarantor of the cataclysm in Iraq. But first I must turn from great things to small, for a paragraph, and talk about writing, and the strange thing that happened to me at my desk in this, the Age of Vanished Normalcy.

All writers of fiction will at some point find themselves abandoning a piece of work—or find themselves "putting it aside," as we gently say. The original idea, the initiating "throb" (Nabokov), encounters certain "points of resistance" (Updike); and these points of resistance, on occasion, are simply too obdurate, numerous, and pervasive. You come to write the next page, and it's dead—as if your subconscious, the part of you quietly responsible for so much daily labor, has been neutralized, or switched off. Norman Mailer has said that one of the few real sorrows of "the spooky art" is that it requires you to spend too many days among dead things. Recently, and for the first time in my life, I abandoned, not a dead thing, but a thriving novella; and I did so for reasons that were wholly extraneous. I am aware that this is hardly a tectonic event; but for me the episode was existential. In the West, writers are acclimatized to freedom—to limitless and gluttonous freedom. And I discovered something. Writing *is* freedom; and as soon as that freedom is in shadow, the writer can no longer proceed. The shadow was not a fear of repercussion. It was as if, most reluctantly, I was receiving a new vibration or frequency from the planetary shimmer. The novella was a satire called "The Unknown Known."

Secretary Rumsfeld was unfairly ridiculed, some thought, for his haiku-like taxonomy of the terrorist threat:

The message is: there are known "knowns." There are things that we know that we know. There are known unknowns. That is to say, there are things that we know we don't know. But there are also unknown unknowns. There are things we don't know we don't know.

Like his habit of talking in "the third person passive once removed," this is "very Rumsfeldian." And Rumsfeld can be even more Rumsfeldian than that. According to Bob Woodward's *Plan of Attack,* at a closed-door senatorial briefing in September 2002 (the idea was to sell regime-change in Iraq), Rumsfeld exasperated everyone present with a torrent of Rumsfeldisms, including the following strophe: "We know what we know, we know there are things we do not know, and we know there are things we know we don't know we don't know." Anyway, the three categories remain quite helpful as analytical tools. And they certainly appealed very powerfully to the narrator of "The Unknown Known"— Ayed, a diminutive Islamist terrorist who plies his trade in Waziristan, the rugged northern borderland where Osama bin Laden is still rumored to lurk.

Ayed's outfit, which is called "the 'Prism,'" used to consist of three sectors named, not very imaginatively, Sector One, Sector Two, and Sector Three. But Ayed and his colleagues are attentive readers of the Western press, and the sectors now have new titles. Known Knowns (Sector One) concerns itself with daily logistics: bombs, mines, shells, and various improvised explosive devices. The work of Known Unknowns (Sector Two) is more peripatetic and long-term; it involves, for example, trolling around North Korea in the hope of procuring the fabled twenty-five kilograms of enriched uranium, or going from factory to factory in Uzbekistan on a quest for better toxins and asphyxiants. In Known Knowns, the brothers are plagued by fires and gas leaks and almost daily explosions; the brothers in Known Unknowns are racked by headaches and sore throats, and their breath, tellingly, is rich with the aroma of potent coughdrops, moving about as they do among vats of acids and bathtubs of raw pesticides. Everyone wants to work where Ayed works, which is in Sector Three, or Unknown Unknowns. Sector Three is devoted to conceptual breakthroughs—to shifts in the paradigm.

Shifts in the paradigm like the attack of September 11, 2001. Paradigm-shifts open a window; and, once opened, the window will close. Ayed observes that September 11 was instantly unrepeatable; indeed, the tactic was obsolete by 10 a.m. the same morning. Its efficacy lasted for seventy-one minutes, from 8:46, when American 11 hit the North Tower, to 9:57, and the start of the rebellion on United 93. On United 93, the passengers were told about the new reality by their mobile phones, and they didn't linger long in the old paradigm—the four-day siege on the equatorial tarmac, the diminishing supplies of food and water, the festering toilets, the conditions and demands, the phased release of the children and the women; then the surrender, or the clambering commandos. No, they knew that they weren't on a commercial aircraft, not any longer; they were on a missile. So they rose up. And at 10:03 United 93 came down on its back at 580 mph, in Shanksville, Pennsylvania, twenty minutes from the Capitol.

I found it reassuringly difficult, dreaming up paradigm-shifts. And Ayed and his friends in Sector Three find it difficult too. Synergy, maximalization—these are the kinds of concepts that are tossed from cushion to floor mat in Unknown Unknowns. Here, a comrade argues for the dynamiting of the San Andreas Fault; there, another envisages the large-scale introduction of rabies (admixed with small-pox, methamphetamine, and steroids) to the fauna of Central Park. A pensive silence follows. And very often these silences last for days on end. All you can hear, in Unknown Unknowns, is the occasional swatting palm-clap, or the crackle of a beetle being ground underfoot. Ayed feels, or used to feel, superior to his colleagues, because he has already had his eureka moment. He had it in the spring of 2001, and his project—his "baby," if you will—was launched in the summer of that year, and is still in progress. It has a code name: UU: CRs/G,C.

Ayed's conceptual breakthrough did not go down at all well in Sector Three, as it was then called; in fact, it was widely mocked. But Ayed used a family connection, and gained an audience with Mullah Omar, the one-eyed Islamist cleric who briefly ruled Afghanistan—an imposing figure, in his dishdash and flipflops. Ayed submitted his presentation, and, to his astonishment, Mullah Omar smiled on his plan. This was a necessary condition, because Ayed's paradigm-shift could only be realized with the full resources of a nation state. UU: CRs/G,C went ahead. The idea was, as Ayed would say, deceptively simple. The idea was to scour all the prisons and madhouses for every compulsive rapist in the country, and then unleash them on Greeley, Colorado.

As the story opens, the CRs have been en route to G,C for almost five years, crossing central Africa, in minibuses and on foot, and suffering many a sanguinary reverse (a host of some thirty thousand Janjaweed in Sudan, a "child militia," armed with pangas, in Congo). On top of all this, as if he didn't have enough to worry about, Ayed is not getting on very well with his wives.

. . .

Those who know the field will be undismayed by the singling out of Greeley, Colorado. For it was in Greeley, Colorado, in 1949, that Islamism, as we now know it, was decisively shaped. The story is grotesque and incredible—but then so are its consequences. And let us keep on telling ourselves how grotesque and incredible it is, our current reality, so unforeseeable, so altogether unknowable, even from the vantage of the late 1990s. In the late 1990s, if you recall, America had so much leisure on its hands, politically and culturally, that it could dedicate an entire year to Monica Lewinsky. Even Monica, it now seems, even Bill, were living in innocent times.

Since then the world has undergone a moral crash—the spiritual equivalent, in its global depth and reach, of the Great Depression of the 1930s. On our side, extraordinary rendition, coercive psychological procedures, enhanced interrogation techniques, Guantánamo, Abu Ghraib, Haditha, Mahmudiya, two wars, and tens of thousands of dead bodies.*

All this should of course be soberly compared to the feats of the opposed ideology, an ideology which, in its most millennial form, conjures up the image of an abattoir within a madhouse. I will spell this out, because it has not been broadly assimilated. The most extreme Sunni Islamists want to kill everyone on earth except the most extreme Sunni

---

* This last figure, we now know, should be drastically revised. In Iraq we have brought about a new kind of hell; and there is no exculpation in the fact that Muslim deaths, in Iraq as elsewhere, are predominantly Muslim on Muslim.

Islamists; but every rank-and-file jihadi sees the need for eliminating all non-Muslims, either by conversion or by execution. And we now know what happens when Islamism gets its hands on an army (Algeria) or on something resembling a nation state (Sudan). In the first case, the result was fratricide, with 100,000 dead; in the second, following the Islamist coup in 1989, the result has been a kind of rolling genocide, and the figure is perhaps two million. And it all goes back to Greeley, Colorado, and to Sayyid Qutb.

Things started to go wrong for Sayyid during the Atlantic crossing from Alexandria, when, allegedly, "a drunken, semi-naked woman" tried to storm his cabin. But before we come to that, some background. Sayyid Qutb, in 1949, had just turned forty-three. His childhood was provincial and devout. When, as a young man, he went to study in Cairo, his leanings became literary and Europhone and even mildly cosmopolitan. Despite an early—and routinely baffling—admiration for naturism, he was already finding Cairene women "dishonorable," and confessed to unhappiness about "their current level of freedom." A short story recorded his first disappointment in matters of the heart; its title, plangently, was "Thorns." Well, we've all had that; and most of us then adhere to the arc described in Peter Porter's poem "Once Bitten, Twice Bitten." But Sayyid didn't need much discouragement. Promptly giving up all hope of coming across a woman of "sufficient" cleanliness, he resolved to stick to the devil he knew: virginity.

Established in a modest way as a writer, Sayyid took a job at the Ministry of Education. This radicalized him. He felt oppressed by the vestiges of the British protectorate in Egypt, and was alarmist about the growing weight of the Jewish presence in Palestine—another British crime, in Sayyid's view. He became an activist, and ran some risk of imprisonment (at the hands of the saturnalian King Farouk), before the ministry packed him off to America to do a couple of years of educational research. Prison, by the way, would claim him soon after his return. He was one of the dozens of Muslim Brothers jailed (and tortured) after the failed attempt on the life of the modernizer and secularist Nasser in October 1954. There was a short reprieve in 1964, but Sayyid was soon rearrested—and retortured. Steelily dismissing a clemency deal brokered by none other than the young Anwar Sadat, he was hanged in August 1966; and this was a strategic martyrdom that now lies deep in the Islamist soul. His most influential book, like the book with which it is often compared, was written behind bars. *Milestones* is known as the *Mein Kampf* of Islamism.

Sayyid was presumably still shaken by the birth of Israel (after the defeat of Egypt and five other Islamic armies), but at first, on the ocean crossing, he felt a spiritual expansion. His encyclopedic commentary, *In the Shade of the Koran,* would fondly and ramblingly recall the renewal of his sense of purpose and destiny. Early on, he got into a minor sectarian battle with a proselytizing Christian; Sayyid retaliated by doing a bit of proselytizing himself, and made some progress with a contingent of Nubian sailors. Then came the traumatic incident with the drunken, semi-naked woman. Sayyid thought she was an American agent hired to seduce him, or so he later told his biographer, who wrote that "the encounter successfully tested his resolve to resist experiences damaging to his identity as an Egyptian and a Muslim." God knows what the episode actually amounted to. It seems probable that the liquored-up Mata Hari, the dipsomaniacal nudist, was simply a woman in a cocktail dress who, perhaps, had recently had a cocktail. Still, we can continue to imagine Sayyid barricading himself into his cabin while, beyond the door, the siren sings her song.

He didn't like New York: materialistic, mechanistic, trivial, idolatrous, wanton, depraved, and so on and so forth. Washington was a little better. But here, sickly Sayyid (lungs) was hospitalized, introducing him to another dire hazard that he wouldn't have faced at home: female nurses. One of them, tricked out with "thirsty lips, bulging breasts, smooth legs" and a coquettish manner ("the calling eye, the provocative laugh"), regaled him with her wish-list of endowments for the ideal lover. But the father of Islamism, as he is often called, remained calm, later developing the incident into a diatribe against Arab men who succumb to the allure of American women. In an extraordinary burst of mendacity or delusion, Sayyid claimed that the medical staff heartlessly exulted at the news of the assassination, back in Egypt, of Hasan al-Banna. We may wonder how likely it is that any American would have heard of the Hitler-fancying al-Banna, or indeed of the Muslim Brotherhood, which he founded. When Sayyid was discharged from George Washington University Hospital, he probably thought the worst was behind him. But now he proceeded to the cauldron—to the pullulating hellhouse—of Greeley, Colorado.

During his six months at the Colorado State College of

Education (and thereafter in California), Sayyid's hungry disapproval found a variety of targets. American *lawns* (a distressing example of selfishness and atomism), American conversation ("money, movie stars and models of cars"), American jazz ("a type of music invented by Blacks to please their primitive tendencies—their desire for noise and their appetite for sexual arousal"), and, of course, American women: here another one pops up, telling Sayyid that sex is merely a physical function, untrammeled by morality. American places of worship he also detests (they are like cinemas or amusement arcades), but by now he is pining for Cairo, and for company, and he does something rash. Qutb joins a club—where an epiphany awaits him. "The dance is inflamed by the notes of the gramophone," he wrote; "the dance hall becomes a whirl of heels and thighs, arms enfold hips, lips and breasts meet, and the air is full of lust." You'd think that the father of Islamism had exposed himself to an early version of Studio 54 or even Plato's Retreat. But no: the club he joined was run by the church, and what he is describing, here, is a chapel hop in Greeley, Colorado. And Greeley, Colorado, in 1949, was *dry*.

"And the air is full of lust." "Lust" is Bernard Lewis's translation, but several other writers prefer the word "love." And while *lust* has greater immediate impact, *love* may in the end be more resonant. Why should Qutb mind if the air is full of love? We are forced to wonder whether love can be said to exist, as we understand it, in the ferocious patriarchy of Islamism. If death and hate are the twin opposites of love, then it may not be merely whimsical and mawkish to suggest that the terrorist, the bringer of death and hate, the death-hate cultist, is in essence the enemy of love. Qutb:

A girl looks at you, appearing as if she were an enchant-
ing nymph or an escaped mermaid, but as she approaches,
you sense only the screaming instinct inside her, and
you can smell her burning body, not the scent of per-
fume but flesh, only flesh.

In his excellent book *Terror and Liberalism,* Paul Berman has
many sharp things to say about the corpus of Sayyid Qutb;
but he manages to goad himself into receptivity, and ends
up, in my view, sounding almost absurdly respectful—"rich,
nuanced, deep, soulful, and heartfelt." Qutb, who would go
on to write a thirty-volume gloss on it, spent his childhood
memorizing the Koran, and on his own initiative. He was ten
by the time he was done. Now, given that, it seems idle to
expect much sense from him; and so it proves. On the last of
the forty-six pages he devotes to Qutb, Berman wraps things
up with a long quotation. This is its repetitive first paragraph:

> The surah [the sayings of the Prophet] tells the Muslims
> that, in the fight to uphold God's universal Truth, lives
> will have to be sacrificed. Those who risk their lives and
> go out to fight, and who are prepared to lay down their
> lives for the cause of God, are honorable people, pure of
> heart and blessed of soul. But the great surprise is that
> those among them who are killed in the struggle must
> not be considered or described as dead. They continue
> to live, as God Himself clearly states.

Savoring that last phrase, we realize that any voyage taken
with Sayyid Qutb is doomed to a leaden-witted circularity.

The emptiness, the mere iteration, at the heart of his philosophy is steadily colonized by a vast entanglement of bitternesses; and here, too, we detect the presence of that peculiarly Islamist triumvirate (codified by Christopher Hitchens) of self-righteousness, self-pity, and self-hatred—the self-righteousness dating from the seventh century, the self-pity from the thirteenth (when the "last" Caliph was kicked to death in Baghdad by the Mongol warlord Hulagu), and the self-hatred from the twentieth. And most astounding of all, in Qutb, is the level of self-awareness, which is less than zero. It is as if the very act of self-examination were something unmanly or profane: something unrighteous, in a word.

Still, one way or the other, Qutb is the father of Islamism. Here are the chief tenets he inspired: that America, and its clients, are *jahiliyyah* (the word classically applied to pre-Muhammadan Arabia—barbarous and benighted); that America is controlled by Jews; that Americans are infidels, that they are animals and, worse, arrogant animals, and are unworthy of life; that America promotes pride and promiscuity in the service of human degradation; that America seeks to "exterminate" Islam—and that it will accomplish this not by conquest, not by colonial annexation, but *by example*. As Bernard Lewis puts it in *The Crisis of Islam*:

> This is what is meant by the term the Great Satan, applied to the United States by the late Ayatollah Khomeini. Satan as depicted in the Qur'an is neither an imperialist nor an exploiter. He is a seducer, "the insidious tempter who whispers in the hearts of men" (Qur'an, CXIV, 4, 5).

Lewis might have added that these are the closing words of the Koran. So they echo.

The West *isn't* being seductive, of course; all the West is being is attractive. But the Islamist's paranoia extends to a kind of thwarted narcissism. We think again of Qutb's buxom, smooth-legged nurse, supposedly smacking her thirsty lips at the news of the death of Hasan al-Banna. Far from wanting or trying to exterminate it, the West had no views whatever about Islam per se before September 11, 2001. Of course, views were then formulated, and very soon the best-seller list was a column of Islamic primers. Some things take longer to sink in than others, true; but now we know. In the West we had brought into being a society whose main purpose, whose *raison d'être,* was the tantalization of good Muslims.

The theme of the "tempter" can be taken a little further, in the case of Qutb. When the tempter is a temptress, and really wants you to sin, she needs to be both available and willing. And it is almost inconceivable that poor Sayyid, the frail, humorless civil servant, and turgid anti-Semite (salting his talk with quotes from that long-exploded fabrication *The Protocols of the Elders of Zion*), ever encountered anything that resembled an offer. It is more pitiful than that. Seduction did not come his way, but it was coming the way of others, he sensed, and a part of him wanted it too. That desire made him very afraid, and also shamed him and dishonored him, and turned his thoughts to murder. Then the thinkers of Islam took his books and did what they did to them; and Sayyid Qutb is now a part of our daily reality. We should understand that the Islamists' hatred of America is as much abstract as historical, and irrationally abstract too; none of the usual things can be expected to appease it. The hatred contains much historical emotion, but it is their history, and not ours, that haunts them.

Qutb has perhaps a single parallel or precedent. Another shambling invert, another sexual truant (not a virgin but a career cuckold), another marginal quack and dabbler (talentless but not philistine), he too wrote a book, in prison, that fell into the worst possible hands. His name was Nikolai Chernyshevsky; and his novel, *What Is to Be Done?*, was read five times by Vladimir Lenin in the course of a single summer. It was Chernyshevsky who determined, not the content, but the emotional dynamic of the Soviet experiment. The centennial of his birth was celebrated with much pomp in the U.S.S.R. That was in 1928. But Russia was too sad, and too busy, to do much about the centennial of his death, which passed quietly in 1989.

In "The Unknown Known," my diminutive terrorist, Ayed, is not a virgin (or a Joseph, as Christians say), unlike Sayyid, on whom he is tangentially based. He is, rather, a polygamist, confining himself to the sanctioned maximum of four. On top of this, he indulges himself, whenever he has enough spare cash, with a succession of "temporary wives." The practice is called *mutah*. In her justly celebrated book, *Reading Lolita in Tehran,* Azar Nafisi tells us that a temporary marriage can endure for ninety-nine years; it can also be over in half an hour. The Islamic Republic of Iran is very attentive to what it calls "men's needs." Before the Revolution, a girl could get married when she turned eighteen. After 1979, the age requirement was halved.

In *Beyond Belief: Islamic Excursions Among the Converted Peoples,* V. S. Naipaul looks at some of the social results of polygamy, in Pakistan, and notes that the marriages tend to be serial. The man moves on, "religiously tom-catting away"; and the consequence is a society of "half-orphans." Divorce is in any case unarduous: "A man who wanted to get rid of his wife could accuse her of adultery and have her imprisoned." In Iraq, doctors attached to the judiciary have said that in the pre-invasion years "virginity testing" was by far the most common procedure they were called upon to perform. It is difficult to exaggerate the sexual invasiveness (in at least two senses) of the Islamic system, even among the figures we think of as moderate. Type "sex and al-Sistani" into the search engine, and prepare yourself for a cataract of pedantry and smut.

As the narrative opens, Ayed is very concerned about the state of his marriages. But there's a reason for that. When Ayed was a little boy, in the early 1980s, his dad, a talented poppy-farmer, left Waziristan with his family and settled in Greeley, Colorado. This results in a domestic blow to Ayed's self-esteem. Back home in Waziristan, a boy of his age would be feeling a lovely warm glow of pride, around now, as he realizes that his sisters, in one important respect, are just like his mother: *they* can't read or write either. In America, though, the girls are obliged to go to school. Before Ayed knows it, the women have shed their veils, and his sisters are being called on by gum-chewing *kafirs*. Now puberty looms.

There is almost an entire literary genre given over to sensibilities such as Sayyid Qutb's. It is the genre of the unreliable narrator—or, more exactly, the transparent narrator, with his helpless giveaways. Typically, a patina of haughty fastidiousness strives confidently but in vain to conceal an underworld of incurable murk. In "The Unknown Known" I added to this genre, and with enthusiasm. I had Ayed stand for hours in a thicket of nettles and poison ivy beneath an elevated walkway, so that he could rail against the airiness of the summer frocks worn by American women and the shameless brevity of their underpants. I had him go out in all weathers for evening strolls, strolls gruelingly prolonged until, with the help of a buttress or a drainpipe, he comes across a woman "quite openly" undressing for bed. Meanwhile, his sisters are all dating. The father and the brothers discuss various courses of action, such as killing them all; but America, bereft of any sense of honor, would punish them for that. The family bifurcates; Ayed returns to the rugged borderland, joins "the 'Prism,'" and courts his quartet of nine-year-old sweethearts. He pops the questions, and ties the knots.

As Ayed keeps telling all his temporary wives, "My wives don't understand me." And they don't; indeed, they all want divorces, and for the same embarrassing reason. With his paradigm-shift attack on America now in ruins, and facing professional and social disgrace, Ayed suddenly sees how, in one swoop, he can redeem himself—and secure his place in history—with an unknown unknown which is sure to succeed. For this he will be needing a *belt*.

. . .

Two years ago I came across a striking photograph in a news magazine: it looked like a crudely cross-sectioned watermelon, but you could make out one or two humanoid features half submerged in the crimson pulp. It was in fact the bravely circularized photograph of the face of a Saudi newscaster who had been beaten by her husband. In an attempted murder, it seems: at the time of his arrest he had her in the trunk of his car, and was evidently taking her into the desert for interment. What had she done to bring this on herself? In the marital home, that night, the telephone rang and the newscaster, a prosperous celebrity in her own right, answered it. She had answered the telephone. Male Westerners will be struck, here, by a dramatic cultural contrast. I know that I, for one, would be far more likely to beat my wife to death if she *hadn't* answered the telephone. But customs and mores vary from country to country, and you cannot reasonably claim that one ethos is "better" than any other.

In 1949 Greeley was dry . . . It has been seriously suggested, by serious commentators, that suicide–mass murderers are searching for the simplest means of getting a girlfriend. It may be, too, that some of them are searching for the simplest means of getting a drink. Although alcohol, like extramarital sex, may be strictly forbidden in life, there is, in death, no shortage of either. As well as the Koranic virgins, "as chaste," for the time being, "as the sheltered eggs of ostriches," there is also a "gushing fountain" of white wine (wine "that will neither pain their heads nor take away their reason"). The suicide–mass murderer can now raise his brimming "goblet" to an additional reward: he has the power, post-mortem, to secure paradisal immortality for a host of relations (the number is a round seventy, two fewer, curiously, than the traditional allotment of houris). Nor is this his only service to the clan, which, until recently, could expect an honorarium of $20,000 from Iraq, plus $5,000 from Saudi Arabia—as well as the vast prestige automatically accorded to the family of a martyr. And then there is the enticement, and incitement, of peer-group prestige.

Suicide–mass murder is astonishingly alien, so alien, in fact, that Western opinion has been unable to formulate a rational response to it. A rational response would be something like an unvarying factory siren of unanimous disgust. But we haven't managed that. What we have managed, on the whole, is a murmur of dissonant evasion. Paul Berman's best chapter in *Terror and Liberalism* is mildly entitled "Wishful Thinking"—and Berman is in general a mild-mannered man. But this is a very tough and persistent analysis of our extraordinary uncertainty. It is impossible to read it without cold fascination and a consciousness of disgrace. I felt disgrace, during its early pages, because I had done it too, and in print, early on. Contemplating intense violence, you very rationally ask yourself, "What are the *reasons* for this?" And compassionately frowning newscasters are still asking that same question. It is time to move on. We are not dealing in reasons because we are not dealing in reason.

After the failure of Oslo, and the attendant consolidation of Hamas, the second intifada ("earthquake") got under way in 2001, not with stonings and stabbings, like the first, but with a steady campaign of suicide–mass murder. "All over the world," writes Berman, "the popularity of the Palestinian cause did not collapse. It increased." The parallel process was the intensive demonization of Israel (academic ostracism, and so on); every act of suicide–mass murder "testified" to the extremity of the oppression, so that "Palestinian terror, in this view, was the measure of Israeli guilt." And when Sharon replaced Barak, and the expected crackdown began, and the Israeli army, with twenty-three casualties of its own, killed fifty-two Palestinians in the West Bank city of Jenin, the assault was seen as

> a veritable Holocaust, an Auschwitz, or, in an alternative image, as the Middle Eastern equivalent of the Wehrmacht's assault on the Warsaw Ghetto. These tropes were massively accepted, around the world. Typing in the combined names of "Jenin" and "Auschwitz" . . . I came up with 2,890 references; and, typing in "Jenin" and "Nazi," I came up with 8,100 references. There were 63,100 references to the combined names of "Sharon" and "Hitler."

Once the redoubled suppression had taken hold, the human bombings decreased; and world opinion quietened down. The Palestinians were now worse off than ever, their societal gains of the 1990s "flattened by Israeli tanks." But the protests "rose and fell in tandem with the suicide-bomb attacks, and not in tandem with the suffering of the Palestinian people."

This was because suicide–mass murder presented the West with a philosophical crisis. The quickest way out of it was to pretend that the tactic was reasonable, indeed logical and even admirable: an extreme case of "rationalist naïveté," in Berman's phrase. Rationalist naïveté was easier than the assimilation of the alternative: that is to say, the existence of a pathological cult. Berman assembles many voices. And if we are going to hear the rhetoric of delusion and self-hypnosis, then we might as well hear it from a Stockholm laureate—the Portuguese novelist José Saramago. Again erring on the side of indulgence, Berman is unnecessarily daunted by the pedigree of Saramago's prose, which is in fact the purest and snootiest bombast (you might call it Nobelese). Here he focuses his high gaze on the phenomenon of suicide–mass murder:

> Ah, yes, the horrendous massacres of civilians caused by the so-called suicide terrorists . . . Horrendous, yes, doubtless; condemnable, yes, doubtless, but Israel still has a lot to learn if it is not capable of understanding the reasons that can bring a human being to turn himself into a bomb.

And the prose itself seems to take a break, at this point, in expectation of the prolonged and stormy applause.

Palestinian society has channeled a good deal of thought and energy into the solemnization of suicide–mass murder, a process which begins in kindergarten. Naturally one would be reluctant to question the cloudless piety of the Palestinian mother who, having raised one suicide–mass murderer, expressed the wish that his younger brother would become a suicide–mass murderer too. But the time has come to cease to respect the quality of her "rage"—to cease to marvel at the unhinging rigor of Israeli oppression—and to start to marvel at the power of an entrenched and emulous ideology. And if oppression is what we're interested in, then we should think of the oppression, not to mention the life expectancy (and, God, *what* a life), of the younger brother. There will be much stopping and starting to do. It is painful to stop believing in the purity, and the sanity, of the underdog. It is painful to start believing in a cult of death, and in an enemy that wants its war to last forever.

Suicide–mass murder is more than terrorism: it is horrorism. It is a maximum malevolence. For the suicide–mass murderer asks his prospective victims to contemplate their fellow human being with a completely new order of execration. It is *not* like looking down the barrel of a gun. We can tell this is so, because we see what happens, sometimes, when the suicide–mass murderer isn't even there—as in the amazingly summary injustice meted out to the Brazilian Jean Charles de Menenez in London. A more startling example was the rumor-ignited bridge stampede in Baghdad (August 31, 2005). This is the superterror inspired by suicide–mass murder: just whisper the words, and you fatally trample a thousand people. And it remains an accurate measure of the Islamists' contortion: they hold that an act of lethal self-bespatterment, in the interests of an unachievable "cause," brings with it the keys to paradise. Sam Harris, in *The End of Faith: Religion, Terror, and the Future of Reason,* stresses just how thoroughly and expeditiously the suicide–mass murderer is "saved." Which would *you* prefer, given belief?

> . . . martyrdom is the only way that a Muslim can bypass
> the painful litigation that awaits us all on the Day of

Judgment and proceed directly to paradise. Rather than spend centuries moldering in the earth in anticipation of being resurrected and subsequently interrogated by wrathful angels, the martyr is immediately transported to Allah's Garden . . .

Osama bin Laden's table talk, at Tarnak Farms in Afghanistan, where he trained his operatives before September 2001, must have included many rolling paragraphs on Western vitiation, corruption, perversion, prostitution, and all the rest. And in 1998, as season after season unfolded around the President's weakness for fellatio, he seemed to have good grounds for his most serious miscalculation: the belief that America was a softer antagonist than the U.S.S.R. (in whose defeat, incidentally, the "Arab Afghans" played a negligible part). Still, a sympathizer like the famously obtuse "American Taliban," John Walker Lindh, if he'd been there, and if he'd been a little brighter, might have framed the following argument.

Now would be a good time to strike, John would tell Osama, because the West is enfeebled, not just by sex and alcohol, but also by thirty years of multicultural relativism. They'll think suicide-bombing is just an exotic foible, like shame-and-honor killings or female circumcision. Besides, it's religious, and they're always slow to question anything that calls itself that. Within days of our opening outrage, the British royals will go on the road for Islam, and stay on it. And you'll be amazed by how long the word "Islamophobia," as an unanswerable indictment, will cover Islamism too. It'll take them years to come up with the word they want—and "Islamismophobia" clearly isn't any good. Even if the

Planes Operation succeeds, and thousands die, the Left will yawn and wonder why we waited so long. Strike now. Whatever we do, the liberals will all be saying that the West had it coming. Their ideology will make them reluctant to see what it is they confront. And it will make them slow learners.

By the summer of 2005, suicide–mass murder had evolved. In Iraq, foreign jihadis, pilgrims of war, were filing across the borders to be strapped up with explosives and nails and nuts and bolts, often by godless Baathists with entirely secular aims — to be primed like pieces of ordnance and then sent out *the same day* to slaughter their fellow Muslims. Suicide–mass murder, in other words, had passed through a phase of decadence and was now on the point of debauchery. In a single month (May), there were more human bombings in Iraq than during the entire intifada. And this, on July 25, was the response of the Mayor of London to the tactic of self-detonation (eighteen days after July 7):

> Given that they don't have jet planes, don't have tanks, they only have their bodies to use as weapons. In an unfair balance, that's what people use.

I remember a miserable little drip of a *poem,* c. 2002, that made exactly the same case. No, they don't have F-16s. Question: would the Mayor *like* them to have F-16s? And, no, their bodies are not what "people" use. They are what Islamists use. And we should weigh, too, the spiritual paltriness of such martyrdoms. "Martyr" means *witness*. The suicide–mass murderer witnesses nothing — and sacrifices nothing. He dies for vulgar and delusive gain. And on another level, too, the rationale for "martyrdom operations" is a theological sophistry, and blackly cynical. Its aim is simply the procurement of delivery systems.

Our ideology, which is sometimes called Westernism, weakens us in two ways. It weakens our powers of perception and judgment, and it weakens our moral unity and will. As Harris puts it:

> Sayyid Qutb, Osama bin Laden's favorite philosopher, felt that pragmatism would spell the death of American civilization . . . Pragmatism, when civilizations come clashing, does not appear likely to be very pragmatic. To lose the conviction that you can actually be right— about *anything*—seems a recipe for the End of Days chaos envisioned by Yeats: when "the best lack all conviction, while the worst are full of passionate intensity."

The opening argument we reach for now, in explaining any conflict, is the argument of moral equivalence. No value can be allowed to stand in stone, so we begin to question our ability to identify even what is *malum per se*. Prison beatings, too, are evil in themselves, and so is the delegation of torture, and murder, to less high-minded and (it has to be said) less hypocritical regimes. In the kind of war that we are now engaged in, an episode like Abu Ghraib is more than a shameful deviation—it is the equivalent of a lost battle. Our moral advantage, still vast and obvious, is not a liability, and we should strengthen and expand it. Like our dependence on reason, it is a strategic strength, and it shores up our legitimacy.

There is another symbiotic overlap between Islamist praxis

and our own, and it is a strange and pitiable one. I mean the drastic elevation of the nonentity. In our popularity-contest culture, with its VIP ciphers and meteoric mediocrities, we understand the attractions of baseless fame—indeed, of instant and meritless immortality. To feel that you are a geo-historical player is a tremendous lure to those condemned, as they see it, to exclusion and anonymity. In its quieter way, this was perhaps the key component of the attraction of West-ern intellectuals to Soviet Communism: "join" and you are suddenly a contributor to planetary events. As Muhammad Atta steered the 767 toward its destination, he was confident, at least, that his fellow town-planners in Aleppo would remember his name, along with everybody else on earth. Sim-ilarly, the ghost of Shehzad Tanweer, as it watched the salvage teams scraping up human remains in the rat-infested crucible beneath the streets of London, could be sure that he had deci-sively outsoared the fish-and-chip shop back in Leeds. And that other great nothingness, Osama bin Laden—he is ever-living.

In July 2005 I flew from Montevideo to New York—and from winter to summer—with my six-year-old daughter and her eight-year-old sister. I drank a beer as I stood in the check-in queue, a practice not frowned on at Carrasco (though it would certainly raise eyebrows at, say, the dedi-cated hajj terminal in Tehran's Maghreb); then we proceeded to security. Now I know that some six-year-old girls can look pretty suspicious; but my youngest daughter isn't like that. She is a slight little blonde with big brown eyes and a quavery voice. Nevertheless, I stood for half an hour at the counter while the official methodically and solemnly searched her carry-on rucksack—staring shrewdly at each story tape and crayon, and palpating the length of all four limbs of her fluffy duck.

There ought to be a better word than *boredom* for the trance of inanition that weaved its way through me. I wanted to say something like, "Even Islamists have not yet started to blow up their own families on airplanes. So please desist until they do. Oh yeah: and stick, for now, to young men who look like they're from the Middle East." The revelations of August 12, 2006 (the plan to destroy ten transatlantic airliners), were more than a year away. And despite the exposure and prevention of their remarkably ambitious hopes, the Walthamstow jihadis did not quite strive in vain. They failed to promote terror, but they won a great symbolic victory for boredom: the banning of books on the seven-hour flight from Britain to America.

My daughters and I arrived safely in New York. In New York, at certain subway stations, the police were searching all the passengers, to thwart terrorism—thus obliging the terrorist to walk the couple of blocks to a subway station where the police *weren't* searching all the passengers. And I couldn't defend myself from a vision of the future; in this future, riding a city bus will be like flying El Al. In the guilty safety of Long Island I watched the TV footage from my hometown, where my other three children live, where I will soon again be living with all five. There were the Londoners, on July 8, going to work on foot, looking stiff and watchful, and taking no pleasure in anything they saw. Eric Hobsbawm got it right in the mid-1990s, when he said that terrorism was part of the atmospheric "pollution" of Western cities. It is a cost-efficient program. Bomb New York and you pollute Madrid; bomb Madrid and you pollute London; bomb London and you pollute Paris and Rome, and repollute New York. But there was the solace given us by the Mayor. No, we should not be surprised by the use of this sempiternal *ruse de guerre*. Using their bodies is what people do.

The age of terror, I suspect, will also be remembered as the age of boredom. Not the kind of boredom that afflicts the blasé and the effete, but a superboredom, rounding out and complementing the superterror of suicide–mass murder. And although we will eventually prevail in the war against terror, or will reduce it, as Mailer says, to "a tolerable level" (this phrase will stick, and will be used by politicians, with quiet pride), we haven't got a chance in the war against boredom. Because boredom is something that the enemy doesn't feel. To be clear: the opposite of religious belief is not atheism or secularism or humanism. It is not an *ism:* it is independence of mind—that's all. When I refer to the age of boredom, I am not thinking of airport queues and subway searches. I mean the global confrontation with the dependent mind.

One way of ending the war on terror would be to capitulate and convert. The transitional period would be a humorless one, no doubt, with stern work to be completed in the city squares, the town centers, and on the village greens. Nevertheless, as the Caliphate is restored in Baghdad, to much joy, the surviving neophytes would soon get used to the voluminous penal code enforced by the Ministry for the Promotion of Virtue and the Suppression of Vice. It would be a world of perfect terror and perfect boredom, and of nothing else—a world with no games, no arts, and no women, a world where the sole entertainment is the public execution. My middle daughter, now aged nine, still believes in imaginary beings (in her case Father Christmas and the Tooth Fairy); so she would have that in common, at least, with her new husband.

Like fundamentalist Judaism and medieval Christianity, Islam is totalist. That is to say, it makes a total claim on the individual. Indeed, there is no individual; there is only the *umma*—the community of believers. Ayatollah Khomeini, in his copious writings, often returns to this theme. He unindulgently notes that believers in most religions appear to think that, so long as they observe all the formal pieties, then for the rest of the time they can do more or less as they please. "Islam," as he frequently reminds us, "isn't like that." Islam follows you everywhere, into the kitchen, into the bedroom, into the bathroom, and beyond death into eternity. Islam means "submission"—the surrender of independence of mind. That surrender now bears the weight of well over fifty generations, and fourteen centuries.

The stout self-sufficiency or, if you prefer, the extreme incuriosity of Islamic culture has been much remarked. Present-day Spain translates as many books into Spanish, annually, as the Arab world has translated into Arabic in the last eleven hundred years. And the medieval Islamic powers barely noticed the existence of the West until they started losing battles to it. The tradition of intellectual autarky was so robust that Islam remained indifferent even to readily available inno-vations, including, incredibly, the wheel. Use of the wheel ceased soon after the emergence of Islam, perhaps as a way of protecting a transport economy based on the camel. I have seen other explanations. The wheel, as we are aware, makes things easier to roll; Bernard Lewis, in *What Went Wrong?*, sagely notes that it also makes things easier to steal.

By the beginning of the twentieth century, in any event, the Muslim countries, with partial exceptions, had been sub-jugated by the European empires. And at that point the doors of perception were opened to a foreign influence: that of Germany. There was no choice—geopolitically, there was nowhere else to turn. This allegiance cost Islam its last imperium, the Ottoman, for decades a "helpless hulk" (Hobsbawm), which was duly dismantled and shared out after the First World War—a war that was made in Berlin. But Islam continued to look to Germany for sponsorship and inspiration. When the Nazi experiment ended, in 1945, sym-pathy for its ideals lingered on for years, but Islam was now forced to look elsewhere. And the flame, again necessarily, passed from Germany to the U.S.S.R.

So Islam, in the end, proved responsive to European influ-ence: the influence of Hitler and Stalin. And one hardly needs to labor the similarities between Islamism and the totalitarian cults of the last century. Anti-Semitic, anti-liberal, anti-individualist, anti-democratic, and, most crucially, anti-rational, they too were cults of death, death-driven and death-fueled. The main distinction is that the paradise which the Nazis (pagan) and the Bolsheviks (atheist) sought to bring about was an earthly one, raised from the mulch of millions of corpses. For them, death was creative, right enough, yet death was still death (as it was for the self-detonating but godless Tamil Tigers). For the Islamists, death is a consummation and a sacrament; death is a beginning. What is worldly life, after all, but "the scum of existence" (Khomeini)? Sam Harris is right:

> Islamism is not merely the latest flavor of totalitarian nihilism. There is a difference between nihilism and a desire for supernatural reward. Islamists could smash the world to atoms and still not be guilty of nihilism, because everything in their world has been transfigured by the light of paradise.

Pathological mass movements are sustained by "dreams of omnipotence and sadism," in Robert Jay Lifton's phrase. That is usually enough. Islamism adds a third inducement to its warriors: a heavenly immortality that begins even before the moment of extinction.

For close to a millennium, Islam could afford to be autarkic. Its rise is one of the wonders of world history—a chain reaction of conquest and conversion, an amassment not just of territory but of millions of hearts and minds. The vigor of its ideal of justice allowed for levels of tolerance significantly higher than those of the West. Culturally, too, Islam was the more evolved. Its assimilations and its learning potentiated the Renaissance—of which, alas, it did not partake. Throughout its ascendancy, Islam was buoyed by what Malise Ruthven, in *A Fury for God,* calls "the argument from manifest success." The fact of expansion underwrote the mandate of heaven.

And now, for the last three or four hundred years, observable reality has propounded a rebuttal: the argument from manifest failure. As one understands it, in the Islamic cosmos there is nothing more painful than the suspicion that something has denatured the covenant with God. This unbearable conclusion must naturally be denied, but it is subliminally present, and accounts, perhaps, for the apocalyptic hurt of the Islamist.

Over the past five years, what we have been witnessing, apart from a moral slump or bust, is a death agony: the death agony of imperial Islam. Islamism is the last wave—the last convulsion. Until 2003, one could take some comfort from the very virulence of the Islamist deformation. Nothing so insanely Dionysian, so impossibly poisonous, could expect to hold itself together over time. In the twentieth century, outside Africa, the only comparable eruptions of death-hunger, of death-estrus, were confined to Nazi Germany and Stalinite Kampuchea, the one lasting twelve years, the other three and a half. Hitler, Pol Pot, Osama: such men only ask to be the last to die. But there are some sound reasons for thinking that the confrontation with Islamism will be testingly prolonged.

It is by now not too difficult to trace what went wrong, psychologically, in the Iraq War. The fatal turn, the fatal forfeiture of legitimacy, came not with the mistaken but also calculated emphasis on Saddam's weapons of mass destruction: the intelligence agencies of every country on earth, Iraq included, believed that he had them. The fatal turn was the American President's all too palpable submission to the intoxicant of power. His walk, his voice, his idiom, right up to his mortifying appearance in the flight suit on the aircraft carrier USS *Abraham Lincoln* ("Mission Accomplished")— every dash and comma in his body language betrayed the unscrupulous confidence of the power surge.

We should parenthetically add that Tony Blair succumbed to it too—with a difference. In "old" Europe, as Rumsfeld haughtily called it, the idea of a political class was predicated on the inculcation of checks and balances, of psychic surge-breakers, to limit the corruption that personal paramountcy always entrains. It was not a matter of mental hygiene; everyone understood that a rotting mind will make rotten decisions. Blair knew this. He also knew that his trump was not a high one: the need of the American people to hear approval for the war in an English accent. Yet there he was, helplessly caught up in the slipstream turbulence of George Bush. Rumsfeld, too, visibly succumbed to it. On television, at this time, he looked as though he had just worked his way through a snowball of cocaine. "Stuff happens," he said, when asked about the looting of the Mesopotamian heritage in Baghdad—the remark of a man not just corrupted but floridly vulgarized by power. As well as the body language, at this time, there was also the language, the power language, all the way from Bush's "I want to kick ass" to his "Bring it on"—a rather blithe incitement, some may now feel, to the armed insurgency.

Contemplating this, one's aversion was very far from being confined to the esthetic. Much followed from it. And we now know that an atmosphere of boosterist unanimity, of pre-war triumphalism, had gathered around the President, an

atmosphere in which any counter-argument, any hint of cir-
cumspection, was seen as a whimper of weakness or disloy-
alty. If she were alive, Barbara Tuchman would be chafing to
write a long addendum to *The March of Folly;* but not even
she could have foreseen a president who, "going into this
period," "was praying for strength to do the Lord's will." A
power rush blessed by God—no, not a good ambience for
precautions and doubts. In 2003, the invasion of Iraq was
presented as a "self-financing" preventive war to enforce dis-
armament and regime-change. Three and a half years later, it
is a misadventure in search of an exit strategy.

The Iraq project was foredoomed by two intrinsic reali-
ties. First, the Middle East is clearly unable, for now, to sustain democratic rule—for the simple reason that its peoples
will vote against it. Did no one whisper the words, in the Situation Room—did no one say what the scholars have been
saying for years? The "electoral policy" of the fundamentalists, writes Lewis, "has been classically summarized as 'One
man (men only), one vote, once.'" Or, in Harris's trope,
democracy will be "little more than a gangplank to theocracy"; and that theocracy will be Islamist. Now the polls
have closed, and the results are coming in, region-wide. In
Lebanon, gains for Hezbollah; in Egypt, gains for Sayyid
Qutb's fraternity, the Muslim Brotherhood; in Palestine, victory for Hamas; in Iran, victory for the soapbox rabble-
rouser and primitive anti-Semite Mahmoud Ahmadinejad.
And in Iraq, a Shia religious coalition. Bush and Blair,
pathetically, had both "hoped" for Allawi, whose return was
14 percent.

Second, Iraq is not a real country. Cobbled together, by

Winston Churchill, in the early 1920s, it consists of three separate (Ottoman) provinces: Sunni, Shia, Kurd—a disposition which looks set to resume. Among the words not listened to by the U.S. Administration, we can include those of Saddam Hussein. Even with an apparatus of terror as savage as any in history, even with chemical weapons, helicopter gunships, and mass killings, even with a proven readiness to cleanse, to displace, and to destroy whole ecosystems, Hussein modestly conceded that he found Iraq a difficult country to keep together. As a Sunni military man put it, Iraqis "hate" Iraq—or "Iraq," a concept that has brought them nothing but suffering. There is no nationalist instinct; the instinct is for atomization.

A third historical reality might also have given us pause. Only the sack of Mecca and Medina, and perhaps Jerusalem, would have caused more pain to the Islamic heart than the taking, and befouling, of the Iraqi capital, the seat of the Caliphate. We have not heard any discussion, at home, about the creedal significance of Baghdad. But we have had some intimations from the jihadi front line. In pronouncements that vibrate with historic afflatus, they speak of their joyful embrace of the chance to meet the infidel in the Land Between the Rivers. It may be that the Coalition has given the enemy a casus belli that will burn for a generation—or for longer, forever, in the dependent mind, which is a mind indifferent to time.

There are vast pluralities all over the West that are thirsting for American failure in Iraq, thirsting for regional conflagration, for a Fertile Crescent bridle-deep in gore—because they hate George Bush. Perhaps they don't realize that they are co-synchronously thirsting for an Islamist victory that will dramatically worsen the lives of their children. And this may come to pass. Let us look at the war, not through bin Laden's eyes, but through the eyes of the cunning of history. From that vantage, September 11 was a provocation. The "slam dunk," the "cakewalk" into Iraq, amounted to a feint, and a trap. And we now know (from five-hundred-page best sellers like *Cobra II* and *Fiasco*) that the invasion of Iraq was quite unbelievably blithe. There was a near-infinity of exploratory research for the occupation, at the level of the subcommittee and the think tank; but when the occupation became a reality, there was no plan.

All the same, we should not delude ourselves that the underlying motives were wholly dishonorable. This is a more complicated, and more familiar, kind of tragedy. The Iraq War represents a gigantic contract, not just for Halliburton, but also for the paving company called Good Intentions. A dramatic (and largely benign) expansion of American power seems to have been the general goal; a dramatic reduction of American power seems to be the general outcome. Iraq was a divagation in what is ominously being called the Long War. To our largely futile losses in blood, treasure, and moral prestige, we can add the loss in time; and time, too, is blood.

An idea presents itself about a better direction to take; and funnily enough its current champion is the daughter of the dark genius behind the current disaster—she is called Liz Cheney. Before we come to that, though, we must briefly return to Ayed, and his belt, and to some quiet thoughts about the art of fiction.

The "belt" ending of "The Unknown Known" came to me fairly late. But the belt was already there, and prominently. All writers will know exactly what this means. It means that the subconscious had made a polite suggestion, a suggestion that the conscious mind had taken a while to see. Ayed's belt, purchased by mail order in Greeley, Colorado, is called a "RodeoMaMa," and consists of a "weight strap" and the pommel of a saddle. Ayed is of that breed of men which holds that a husband should have sex with his wives every night. And his invariable use of the "Rodeo-MaMa" is one of the reasons for the rumble of mutiny in his marriages.

Looking in at the sector of "the 'Prism'" called Known Knowns, Ayed retools his "RodeoMaMa." He goes back to the house and summons his wives—for the last time. Thus Ayed gets his conceptual breakthrough, his unknown unknown: he is the first to bring martyrdom operations into the setting of his own home.

I could write a piece almost as long as this one about why I abandoned "The Unknown Known." The confirmatory moment came a few weeks ago: the freshly fortified suspicion that there exists on our planet a kind of human being who will become a Muslim in order to pursue suicide–mass murder. For quite a time I have felt that Islamism was trying to poison the world; and here was a sign that the poison might take—might mutate, like bird flu. Islam, as I said, is a total system, and like all such systems it is eerily amenable to satire. But with Islamism, with total malignancy, with total terror and total boredom, irony, even militant irony (which is what satire is), merely shrivels and dies.

In *Twentieth Century* the late historian J. M. Roberts took an unsentimental line on the Chinese Revolution:

> More than two thousand years of remarkable historical continuities lie behind that . . . upheaval which, for all its cost and cruelty, was a heroic endeavor, matched in scale only by such gigantic upheavals as the spread of Islam, or Europe's assault on the world in early modern times.

The cost and cruelty, according to Jung Chang and Jon Halliday's *Mao: The Unknown Story,* amounted, perhaps, to seventy million lives. Yet this has to be balanced against "the weight of the past"—nowhere heavier than in China:

> Deliberate attacks on family authority . . . were not merely attempts by a suspicious regime to encourage informers and delation, but attacks on the most conservative of all Chinese institutions. Similarly, the advancement of women and propaganda to discourage early marriage had dimensions going beyond "progressive" feminist ideas or population control; they were an assault on the past such as no other revolution had ever made, for in China the past meant a role for women far inferior to those of pre-revolutionary America, France or even Russia.

There is no momentum, in Islam, for a reformation. And there is no time, now, for a leisurely, slow-lob enlightenment. The necessary upheaval is a revolution—the liberation of women. This will not be the work of a decade or even a generation. Islam is a millennium younger than China. But we should remind ourselves that the Chinese Revolution took half a century to roll through all its villages.

In 2002 the aggregate GDP of the Arab countries was less than the GDP of Spain; and the Islamic states lag behind the West, and the Far East, in every index of industrial and manufacturing output, job creation, technology, literacy, life expectancy, human development, and intellectual vitality. (A recondite example: in terms of the ownership of telephone lines, the leading Islamic nation is the U.A.E., listed in thirty-third place, between Réunion and Macau.) Then, too, there are the matters of tyranny, corruption, and the absence of civil rights and civil society. We may wonder how the Islamists feel when they compare India to Pakistan, one a burgeoning democratic superpower, the other barely distinguishable from a failed state. "What Went Wrong?" asked Bernard Lewis, at book length. Institutionalized irrationalism is the broad answer; and the particular focus, perhaps, is the obscure logic that denies the Islamic world the talent and energy of half its population. No doubt the impulse toward rational inquiry is by now very weak in the rank and file of the Muslim male. But we can dwell on the memory of those images from Afghanistan: the great waves of women hurrying off to school.

The connection between manifest failure and the suppres-

sion of women is unignorable. And you sometimes feel that
the current crux, with its welter of insecurities and nostal-
gias, is little more than a pre-emptive rage — to ward off the
evacuation of the last sanctum of male power. What would
happen if we spent some of the *next* three hundred billion
dollars (this is Liz Cheney's thrust) on the raising of consciousness in the Islamic world? The effect would be inherently
explosive, because the dominion of the male is Koranic — the
unfalsifiable word of God, as dictated to the Prophet:

> Men have authority over women because God has made
> the one superior to the other, and because they spend
> their wealth to maintain them. Good women are obedi-
> ent. They guard their unseen parts because God has
> guarded them. As for those from whom you fear dis-
> obedience, admonish them, forsake them in beds apart,
> and beat them. Then if they obey you, take no further
> action against them. Surely God is high, supreme (4:34).

Can we imagine seeing men on the march in defense of their
right to beat their wives? And if we do see it, then what?
Would *that* win hearts and minds? The martyrs of the
required revolution would be sustained by two obvious
truths: the binding authority of scripture, all over the world,
is very seriously questioned; and women, by definition, are
not a minority. They would know, too, that their struggle is
a heroic assault on the weight of the past — the alpweight of
fourteen centuries.

.   .   .

Attentive readers may have asked themselves what it is, this ridiculous category, the *unknown known*. The unknown known is paradise, scriptural inerrancy, God. The unknown known is religious belief.

All religions are violent; and all ideologies are violent. Even Westernism, so impeccably bland, has violence glinting within it. This is because any belief system involves a degree of illusion, and therefore cannot be defended by mind alone. When challenged, or affronted, the believer's response is hormonal; and the subsequent collision will be one between a brain and a cat's cradle of glands. I will never forget the look on the gatekeeper's face, at the Dome of the Rock in Jerusalem, when I suggested, perhaps rather airily, that he skip some calendric prohibition and let me in anyway. His expression, previously cordial and cold, became a mask; and the mask was saying that killing me, my wife, and my children was something for which he now had warrant. I knew then that the phrase "deeply religious" was a grave abuse of that adverb. Something isn't deep just because it's all that is there; it is more like a varnish on a vacuum. Millennial Islamism is an ideology superimposed upon a religion— illusion upon illusion. It is not merely violent in tendency. Violence is all that is there.

In Philip Larkin's "Aubade" (1977), the poet, on waking, contemplates "unresting death, a whole day nearer now":

> This is a special way of being afraid
> No trick dispels. Religion used to try,
> That vast moth-eaten musical brocade
> Created to pretend we never die . . .

Much earlier, in "Church Going" (1954), examining his habit of visiting country churches and the feelings they arouse in him (chiefly bafflement and boredom), he was able to frame a more expansive response:

> It pleases me to stand in silence here;
>
> A serious house on serious earth it is,
> In whose blent air all our compulsions meet,
> Are recognised, and robed as destinies.
> And that much never can be obsolete,
> Since someone will forever be surprising
> A hunger in himself to be more serious,
> And gravitating with it to this ground,
> Which, he once heard, was proper to grow wise in,
> If only that so many dead lie round.

This is beautifully arrived at. It contains everything that can be decently and rationally said.

We allow that, in the case of religion, or the belief in supernatural beings, the past weighs in, not at two thousand years, but at approximately five million. Even so, the time has come for a measure of impatience in our dealings with those who would take an innocent personal pronoun (which was just minding its own business) and exalt it with a capital letter. Opposition to religion already occupies the high ground, intellectually and morally. People of independent mind should now start to claim the spiritual high ground, too. We should be with Joseph Conrad:

The world of the living contains enough marvels and mysteries as it is—marvels and mysteries acting upon our emotions and intelligence in ways so inexplicable that it would almost justify the conception of life as an enchanted state. No, I am too firm in my consciousness of the marvelous to be ever fascinated by the mere supernatural, which (take it any way you like) is but a manufactured article, the fabrication of minds insensitive to the intimate delicacies of our relation to the dead and to the living, in their countless multitudes; a desecration of our tenderest memories; an outrage on our dignity.

Whatever my native modesty may be it will never condescend to seek help for my imagination within those vain imaginings common to all ages and that in themselves are enough to fill all lovers of mankind with unutterable sadness.

(Author's Note to *The Shadow-Line,* 1920)

SEPTEMBER 2006. *The Observer*

"The Last Days of
Muhammad Atta"

No physical, documentary, or analytical evidence provides a convincing explanation of why [Muhammad] Atta and [Abdulaziz al-]Omari drove to Portland, Maine, from Boston on the morning of September 10, only to return to Logan on Flight 5930 on the morning of September 11.

— The 9/11 Commission Report

1

On September 11, 2001, he opened his eyes at 4 a.m., in Portland, Maine; and Muhammad Atta's last day began.

What was the scene of this awakening? A room in a hotel, of the type designated as "budget" in his guidebook—one up from "basic." It was a Repose Inn, part of a chain. But it wasn't like the other Repose Inns he had lodged at: brisk, hygienic establishments. This place was ponderous and labyrinthine, and as elderly as most of its clientele. And it was cheap. So. The padded nylon quilt as weighty as a lead vest; the big cuboid television on the dresser opposite; and the dented white fridge—where, as it happened, Muhammad Atta's reason for coming to Portland, Maine, lay cooling on its shelf. The particular frugality of these final weeks was part of a peer-group piety contest that he was laconically going along with. Like the others, he was attending to his prayers, disbursing his alms, washing often, eating little, sleeping little. (But he wasn't like the others.) Days earlier, their surplus operational funds—about $26,000—had been abstemiously wired back to the go-between in Dubai.

He slid from the bed and called Abdulaziz, who was already stirring, and perhaps already praying, in the room next door. Then to the shower and the water closet: the chore of ablution, the ordeal of excretion, the torment of depilation. He activated the shower nozzle and removed his undershorts. He stepped within, submitting to the cold and clammy caress of the plastic curtain on his calf and thigh. Then he spent an unbelievably long time trying to remove a hair from the bar of soap; the alien strand kept changing its shape—question mark, infinity symbol—but stayed in place; and the bar of soap, no bigger than a bookmatch when he began, barely existed when he finished. Next, as sometimes happens in these old, massive, and essentially well-intentioned and broad-handed hotels, the water gave a gulp and then turned, in an instant, from a tepid trickle to a molten blast; and as he struggled from the stall he trod on a leaking shampoo sachet and fell heavily and sharply on his coccyx. He had to kick himself out through the steam, and rasped his head on the shower's serrated metal sill. After a while he slowly climbed to his feet and stood there, hands on hips, eyes only lightly closed, head bowed, awaiting recovery. He dried himself with the thin white towel, catching a hangnail in its shine.

Now, emitting a sigh of unqualified grimness, he crouched on the bowl. He didn't even bother with his usual scowling and straining and shuddering, partly because his head felt dangerously engorged. More saliently, he had not moved his bowels since May. In general his upper body was impressively lean, from all the hours in the gym with the "muscle" Saudis; but now there was a solemn mound where his abdominals used to be, as taut and proud as a four-month pregnancy. Nor was this the only sequela. He had a feverish and unvarying ache, not in his gut but in his lower back, his pelvic saddle, and his scrotum. Every few minutes he was required to wait out an interlude of nausea, while disused gastric juices bubbled up in the sump of his throat. His breath smelled like a blighted river.

The worst was yet to come: shaving. Shaving was the worst because it necessarily involved him in the contemplation of his own face. He looked downward while he lathered his cheeks, but then the chin came up and there it was, revealed in vertical strips: the face of Muhammad Atta. Two years ago he had said goodbye to his beard, after Afghanistan. Tangled and oblong and slightly off-center, it had had the effect of softening the disgusted lineaments of the mouth, and it had wholly concealed the frank animus of the underbite. His insides were seized, but his face was somehow incontinent, or so Muhammad Atta felt. The detestation, the detestation of everything, was being sculpted on it, from within. He was amazed that he was still allowed to walk the streets, let alone enter a building or board a plane. Another day, one more day, and they wouldn't let him. Why didn't everybody point, why didn't they cringe, why didn't they run? And yet this face, by now almost comically malevolent, would soon be smiled at, and perfunctorily fussed over (his ticket was business class), by the doomed stewardess.

A hypothesis. If he stood down from the Planes Operation, and it went ahead without him (or if he somehow survived it), he would never be able to travel by air in the United States or anywhere else—not by air, not by train, not by boat, not by bus. The profiling wouldn't need to be racial; it would be facial, merely. No sane man or woman would ever agree to be confined in his vicinity. With that face, growing more gangrenous by the day. And that name, the name he journeyed through life under, itself like a promise of vengeance: Muhammad Atta.

In the last decade, only one human being had taken obvious pleasure from setting eyes on him, and that was the Sheikh. It happened at their introductory meeting, in Kandahar—where, within a matter of minutes, the Sheikh appointed him operational leader. Muhammad Atta knew that the first thing he would be asked was whether he was prepared to die. But the Sheikh was smiling, almost with eyes of love, when he said it. "The question isn't necessary," he began. "I see the answer in your face."

Their Coglan Air commuter flight to Logan was scheduled to leave at six. So he had an hour. He put on his clothes (the dark blue shirt, the black slacks), and settled himself at the dresser, awkwardly, his legs out to one side. Two documents lay before him. He yawned, then sneezed. While shaving, Muhammad Atta, for the first time in his life, had cut himself on the lip (the lower); with surprising speed the gash settled into a convincing imitation of a cold sore. Much less unusually, he had also nicked the fleshy volute of his right nostril, releasing an apparently endless supply of blood; he kept having to get up and fetch more tissues, leaving after him a paper trail of the staunched gouts. The themes of recurrence and prolongation, he sensed, were already beginning to associate themselves with his last day.

Document number one was emblazoned on the screen of his laptop. It was his will and testament, composed in April 1996, when the thoughts of the group had turned to Chechnya. Two Moroccan friends, Mounir and Abdelghani, both devout, had been his witnesses, so he had included a fair amount of formulaic sanctimony. Any old thing would do. "During my funeral, I want everyone to be quiet because God mentioned that he likes being quiet on three occasions: when you read the Koran, during the funeral, and also when you are crawling." Crawling? Had he mistyped? Another provision stared out at him, and further deepened his frown: "The person who will wash my body near my genitals must wear gloves on his hands so he won't touch my genitals." And this: "I don't want pregnant women or a person who is not clean to come and say goodbye to me because I don't approve of it." Well, these anxieties were now academic. No one would say goodbye to him. No one would wash him. No one would touch his genitals.

There was another document on the table, a four-page book-

let in Arabic, put together by the Information Office in Kandahar (and bound by a grimy tassel). Each of them had been given
one; the others would often produce their personal copy and
nod and sway and mutter over it for hour after hour. But
Muhammad Atta wasn't like the others (and he was paying a
price for it). He had barely glanced at the thing until now. "Pull
your shoelaces tight and wear tight socks that grip the shoes and
do not come out of them." He supposed that this was sound
advice. "Let every one of you sharpen his knife and bring about
comfort and relief of his slaughter." A reference, presumably,
to what would happen to the pilots, the first officers, the flight
attendants. Some of the Saudis, they said, had butchered sheep
and camels at Khaldan, the training camp near Kabul. Muhammad Atta did not expect to relish that part of it: the exemplary
use of the box cutters. He pictured the women, in their uni-
forms, in their open-necked shirts. He did not expect to like it;
he did not expect to like death in that form.

Now he sat back, and felt the approach of nausea: it gathered round him, then sifted through him. His mind, inas-
much as it was separable from his body, was close to the
"complete tranquillity" praised and recommended by Kandahar. A very different kind of thirty-three-year-old might
have felt the same tranced surety while contemplating an
afternoon in a borrowed apartment with his true love (and
sexual obsession). But Muhammad Atta's mind and his
body were not separable: this was the difficulty; this was
the mind–body problem—in his case fantastically acute.
Muhammad Atta wasn't like the others, because he was doing
what he was doing for the core reason. The others were
doing what they were doing for the core reason too, but they

had achieved sublimation, by means of jihadi ardor; and their bodies had been convinced by this arrangement and had gone along with it. They ate, drank, smoked, smiled, snored; they took the stairs two at a time. Muhammad Atta's body had not gone along with it. He was doing what he was doing for the core reason and for the core reason only.

"Purify your heart and cleanse it of stains. Forget and be oblivious to the thing which is called World." Muhammad Atta was not religious; he was not even especially political. He had allied himself with the militants because jihad was, by many magnitudes, the most charismatic idea of his generation. To unite ferocity and rectitude in a single word: nothing could compete with that. He played along with it, and did the things that impressed his peers; he collected quotations, citations, charities, pilgrimages, conspiracy theories, and so on, as other people collected autographs or beer mats. And it suited his character. If you took away all the rubbish about faith, then fundamentalism suited his character, and with an almost sinister precision.

For example, the approach to the question of women: he found the blend of aggression and alarmism highly congenial. In addition, he liked the idea of the brotherhood, although of course he exhaustively despised the current contingent, particularly his fellow pilots: Hani (the Pentagon) he barely knew, but he was continuously enraged by Marwan (the other Twin Tower) and almost fascinated by the pitch of his loathing for Ziad (the Capitol) . . . Adultery punished by whipping, sodomy by burial alive: this seemed about right to Muhammad Atta. He also joined in the hatred of music. And the hatred of laughter. "Why do you never laugh?" he was sometimes asked. Ziad would answer, "How can you laugh when people are dying in Palestine?" Muhammad Atta never laughed, not because people were dying in Palestine, but because he found nothing funny. "The thing which is called World." That, too, spoke to him. World had always felt like an illusion—an unreal mockery.

"The time between you and your marriage in heaven is very short." Ah yes, the virgins: six dozen of them—half a gross. Muhammad Atta, with his two degrees in architecture, his excellent English, his excellent German: Muhammad Atta did not believe in the virgins, did not believe in the Garden. How could he believe in such an implausibly, and dauntingly, priapic paradise? He was an apostate: that's what he was. He didn't expect paradise. What he expected was oblivion. And, strange to say, he would find neither.

He packed. He paused and stooped over the dented refrigerator, then straightened up and headed for the door.

In its descent the elevator, with a succession of long-suffering sighs and flabby, juddering curtseys, stopped at the twelfth, the eleventh, the tenth, the ninth, the eighth, the seventh, the sixth, the fifth, the fourth, the third, and the second floors. Old people, their faces flickering with distrust, inched in and out; while they did so, one of their number would press the open-doors button with a defiant, Marfanic thumb. And at this hour too: it was barely light. Muhammad Atta briefly horrified himself with the notion that they were all lovers, returning early to their beds. But no: it must be the sleeplessness, the insomnia of age—the dawn vigils of age. Their efforts to stay alive, in any case, struck him as essentially ignoble. He had felt the same way in the hospital the night before, when he went to see the imam . . . Consulting his watch every ten or fifteen seconds, he decided that this downward journey was dead time, as dead as time could be, like queueing, or an interminable red light, or staring stupidly at the baggage on an airport carousel. He stood there, hemmed in by pallor and decay, and martyred by compound revulsions.

Abdulaziz was waiting for him in the weak glow and piped music of the lobby. Wordless, breakfastless, they joined the line for checkout. More dead time passed. As they fell into step and proceeded through the last of the night to the parking lot, Muhammad Atta, in no very generous spirit, considered his colleague. This particular muscle Saudi seemed as limply calflike as Ahmed al-Nami—the prettyboy in Ziad's platoon. On the other hand, Abdulaziz, with his softly African face, his childish eyes, was almost insultingly easy to dominate. He had a wife and daughter in southern Saudi Arabia. But this was like saying that he had a flatbed truck in southern Saudi Arabia, so little did it appear to weigh on him. He knew the Koran by heart and had also performed certain prayer-leading duties at his local mosque. And yet it was Abdulaziz, and not the apostate, who carried the knife, Abdulaziz who was ready to apply it to the flesh of the stewardess.

When they reached their car Abdulaziz said a few words in praise of God, adding, with some attempt at panache, "So, let us begin our 'architectural studies.'"

Muhammad Atta felt his body give an involuntary jolt. "Who told you?" he said.

"Ziad."

They loaded up and then bent themselves into the front seats.

Abdulaziz wasn't supposed to know about that—about the target code. "Law" was the Capitol. "Politics" was the White House. In the discussions with the Sheikh there had been firm concurrence about "architecture" (the World Trade Center) and "arts" (the Pentagon); but they had disagreed about an altogether different kind of target, namely "electrical engineering." This was the nuclear power plant that Muhammad Atta had seen on one of his training flights near New York. Puzzlingly, the Sheikh withheld his blessing—despite the presumably attractive possibility of turning large swathes of the Eastern Seaboard into a plutonium cemetery for the next seventy millennia (that is, until the year 72001). The Sheikh gave his reasons (restricted airspace, no "symbolic value"). But Muhammad Atta sensed a moral qualm, a silent suggestion that such a move could be considered exorbitant. It was the first and only indication that, in their cosmic war against God's enemies, there was any kind of upper limit. Muhammad Atta often asked himself: Was the *Sheikh* prepared to die? In the course of their conversations it had emerged that, while plainly reconciled to eventual martyrdom (he would have it no other way, and so on), the Sheikh felt little personal attraction to death; and he would soon be additionally famous, Muhammad Atta prophesied, for the strenuousness with which he eluded it.

These meetings and discussions—with the Sheikh and, later, with his Yemeni emissary, Ramzi bin al-Shibh—now lost weight and value in Muhammad Atta's mind, tarnished by Ziad's indiscipline, by Ziad's promiscuity (and if Abdulaziz knew, then all the Saudis knew). He thought back to his historic conversation with Ramzi, on the telephone, in the third week of August.

"Our friend is anxious to know when your course will begin."

"It will be more interesting to study 'law' when Congress has convened."

"But we shouldn't delay. With so many of our students in the U.S. . . ."

"All right. Two branches, an oblique stroke, and a lollipop."

Ramzi called him back and said,

"To be clear. The eleventh of the ninth?"

"Yes," confirmed Muhammad Atta. And he was the first person on earth to say it—to say in that way: "Nine eleven. September the eleventh."

He had cherished the secret until September 9. Now of course everyone knew: the day itself had come. He was impatient for his talk on the phone with Ziad, scheduled for 7 a.m. at Logan. Ziad was still claiming that he hadn't yet decided between "law" and "politics." It looked like "law." As a target, the President's house had lost much of its appeal when they established, insofar as they could, that the President wouldn't be in it.

At that moment the President was readying himself for an early-morning run in Sarasota, Florida, where Muhammad Atta had been taught how to fly, at Jones Aviation, in September 2000.

It was during the drive to Portland International Jetport that the headache began. In recent months he had become something of a connoisseur of headaches. And yet those earlier headaches, it now seemed, were barely worth the name: *this* was what a headache was. At first he attributed its virulence to his misadventure in the shower stall; but then the pain pushed forward over his crown and established itself, like an electric eel, from ear to ear, then from eye to eye—and then both. He had two headaches, not one; and they were apparently at war. The automobile, a Nissan Altima, was brand-new, factory-fresh, and this had seemed like a mild bonus on September 10; but now its vacuum-packed breath tasted of seasickness and the smell of ships below the waterline. Suddenly his vision became pixelated with little swarms of blind spots. So it was then asked of him to pull over and tell an astonished Abdulaziz to take the wheel.

There seemed to be a completely unreasonable weight of traffic. Americans, already about their business . . . Tormenting his passenger with regular glances of concern, Abdulaziz otherwise drove with his usual superstitious watchfulness, beset by small fears, on this day. Muhammad Atta tried not to writhe around in his seat; on his way to the car park, ten minutes earlier, he had tried not to run; in the elevator, ten minutes earlier still, he had tried not to groan or scream. He was always trying not to do something.

It was 5:35 a.m. And at this point he began to belabor himself for the diversion to Portland: a puerile undertaking, as he now saw it. His group was competitive not only in piety but also in nihilistic élan, in nihilistic insouciance; and he had thought it would be conclusively stylish to stroll from one end of Logan to the other with less than an hour to go. Then, too, there was the promise, itchier to the heart than ever, of his conversation with Ziad. But his reason for coming to Portland had been fundamentally unserious. He wouldn't have done it if the Internet, on September 10, had not assured him so repeatedly that it was going to be a flawless morning on September 11.

And he didn't solace himself with the thought that this was, after all, September 11: you could still get to airports without much time to spare.

"Did you pack these bags yourself?"

Muhammad Atta's hand crept toward his brow. "Yes," he said.

"Have they been with you at all times?"

"Yes."

"Did anyone ask you to carry anything for them?"

"No. Is the flight on time?"

"You should make your connection."

"And the bags will go straight through."

"No, sir. You'll need to recheck them at Logan."

"You mean I'll have to go through all this *again*?"

Whatever else terrorism had achieved in the past few decades, it had certainly brought about a net increase in world boredom. It didn't take very long to ask and answer those three questions—about fifteen seconds. But those dead-time questions and answers were repeated, without any variation whatever, hundreds of thousands of times a day. If the Planes Operation went ahead as planned, Muhammad Atta would bequeath more, perhaps much more, dead time, planet-wide. It was appropriate, perhaps, and not paradoxical, that terror should also sharply promote its most obvious opposite. Boredom.

As it happened, Muhammad Atta was a selectee of the

Computer Assisted Passenger Prescreening System (CAPPS). All it meant was that his checked bag would not be stowed until he himself had boarded the aircraft. This was at Portland. At Logan, a "Category X" airport like Newark International and Washington Dulles, and supposedly more secure, three of his muscle Saudis would be selected by CAPPS, with the same irrelevant consequences.

Muhammad Atta and Abdulaziz submitted to the checkpoint screening. Their bags were not searched; they were not frisked, or blessed by the hand wand. Abdulaziz's childish rucksack, containing the box cutters and the Mace, passed through the tunnel of love. Just before boarding, another gust of nausea gathered about Muhammad Atta, like a host of tiny myrmidons. He waited for them to move on, but they did not do so, and, instead, coagulated in his craw. Muhammad Atta went to the men's room and released a fathom of bilious green. He was still wiping his foul mouth as he walked out on to the tarmac and climbed the trembling metal steps.

Coglan 5930 was not only late: it was also an open-propeller nineteen-seater, and it was full. Excruciatingly, he had to wedge himself in next to a fat blonde with a scalp disease and, moreover, a baby, whose incredulous weeping (its ears) she attempted and failed to slake with repeated applications of the breast. Between heartbeats, when he was briefly capable of consecutive thought, he imagined that the blonde was the doomed stewardess.

The plane leapt eagerly into the air, with none of the technological toil that would characterize the ascent of American 11.

. . .

He had gone to Portland, Maine, for his quid pro quo with the imam.

The hospital, where he lay dying, was a blistered medium-rise downtown: one more business among all the other businesses. Inside, too, Muhammad Atta had no sense of entering an atmosphere of vocational care—just the American matter-of-factness, with no softening of the voice, the tread, no softening of the receptionists' minimal smiles . . . Directed to the hospice unit, he moved through the moist warmth of half-eaten or untouched dinners and the heavier undersmell of drugs. The imam was asleep in his bed, recessed into it, as if an imam-sized channel had been let into the mattress. His lips, Muhammad Atta noticed, were dark gray, like the lips of dogs. Dead time passed. Then the imam awoke to Muhammad Atta's unsmiling stare. He sighed, without restraint. The two of them went back a way: to the mosque in Falls Church, Virginia.

"You have a citation for me?" asked the imam, unexpectedly alert.

"It's from the traditions. The Prophet said: 'Whoever kills himself with a blade will be tormented with that blade in the fires of Hell . . . He who throws himself off a mountain and kills himself will throw himself downward into the fires of Hell forever and ever . . . Whoever kills himself in any way in this world will be tormented in that way in Hell.'"

"Always there are exceptions. Remember we are in the lands of unbelief," said the imam, and went on to list the crimes of the Americans.

These were familiar to his visitor, who regarded the griev-ances as real. Depending on how you tallied it, America was responsible for this or that many million deaths. But Muhammad Atta was not persuaded of a moral equivalence. Certain weapons systems claimed to be precise; power was not precise. Power was always a monster. And there had never been a monster the size of America. Every time it turned over in its sleep it entrained disasters that would need to roll through villages. There were blunderings and perversities and calculated cruelties; and there was no self-knowledge—none. Still, America did not expend *ingenuity* in its efforts to kill the innocent.

"Is it an enemy installation?" the imam was sharply asking.

Muhammad Atta gave no reply. He just said, "Do you have it?"

"Yes. And you will need it."

The imam's hand, to Muhammad Atta's far from sympa-thetic gaze, looked and sounded like the foreclaw of a lobster as it rattled up against the laminate of his bedside table. Its cupboard opened, drawbridge-wise. The thing within exactly resembled a half-empty eight-ounce bottle of Volvic.

"Take it, not on waking, but when you feel your trial is near. Now. You were kind enough to say you would describe your induction."

Here was the quid pro quo: he wanted to be told about the Sheikh. Just then the imam abruptly turned on to his side, facing Muhammad Atta; and for a moment his posture repul-sively recalled that of a child starting to warm to a bedtime story. But this lurch was only part of a larger maneuver of the imam's. He edged himself backward and upward, so that a few stray hairs, at least, rested on the pillow.

Muhammad Atta had unthinkingly assumed, earlier on, that he would give the imam a reassuring, even an idealized portrait of the Sheikh—the long-fingered visionary on the mountaintop who yet, in his humility and asceticism, remained a simple warrior of God. Now he recomposed himself. Never in his life had he spoken his mind. The smell of drugs was particularly strong near the yellow sink, half a yard from his nose.

"I had several meetings with him," he said, "at al-Faruq in Kandahar. And at Tarnak Farms. He casts the spell of success on you—that's what he does. When he talks about the defeat of the Russians . . . To hear him tell it, it wasn't the West that won the Cold War. It was the Sheikh. But we badly need that spell, don't we? The spell of success."

"But the successes are real. And this is only the beginning."

"His hopes of victory depend," said Muhammad Atta, "on the active participation of the superpower."

"What superpower?"

"God. Hence the present crisis."

"Meaning?"

"It comes from religious hurt, don't you think? For centuries God has forsaken the believers, and rewarded the infidels. How do *you* explain his indifference?"

Or his enmity, he thought, as he left the bedside and the ward. He considered, too, that it could go like this, subconsciously, of course: if prayer and piety had failed, had so clearly failed, then it might seem time to change allegiance, and summon up the other powers.

.   .   .

At Logan, he and Abdulaziz were the only passengers at the carousel supposedly serving the commuter flight from Portland. And the carousel was silent and motionless. Staring at a carousel with actual baggage going round on it suddenly seemed a fairly stimulating thing to do. Meanwhile, the eels or stingrays in his head were now having a fight to the death in the area just behind his ears. Sometimes for moments on end he could step back from the pain and just *listen* to it. This was music in its next evolutionary phase, beyond the atonal. And he realized why he had always hated music; all of it, even the most emollient melody, had entered his mind as pain. Using every reserve, he continued to stare at the changeless slats of black rubber for another thirty seconds, another minute; then he turned on his heel, and Abdulaziz followed.

"Did you pack these bags yourself?"

"*What* bags? As I took the trouble to explain—"

"Sir, your bags will be on our next flight. I still need to ask the security questions, sir."

Americans—the way they called you "sir." They might as well be calling you "Mac."

"Did you pack these bags yourself?"

"*What* bags?"

Oh, the misery of recurrence, like the hotel elevator doing its ancient kneebend on every floor, like the alien hair on the soap changing its shape through a succession of different alphabets, like the (necessarily) monotonous gonging inside his head. It had occurred to him before that his condition, if you could call it that, was merely the condition of boredom, unbounded boredom, where all time was dead time. As if his whole life consisted of answering those same three questions, saying "Yes" and "Yes" and "No."

"And did anyone ask you to carry anything for them?"

"Yes," said Muhammad Atta. "Last night, at the Lebanese restaurant, a waiter asked us to take a heavy clock radio to his cousin in Los Angeles."

Her smile was flat and brief. "That's funny," she said.

They made their way to Gate 32 and then retreated from it, into the mall. With a flip of the hand he told Abdulaziz to go and look for his countrymen. Muhammad Atta took a seat outside a dormant coffee shop and readied himself for the call to Ziad. Ziad: the Beiruti beach boy and disco ghost, the tippler and debauchee, now with his exaltations and prostrations, his chanting and wailing, his rocking and swaying . . . To discountenance Ziad, to send him to his death with a heart full of doubt: *this* was the reason for the journey to Maine.

Back in Germany, once, Ziad had said that the brides in the Garden would be "made of light." In bold contrast, then, to the darkness and heaviness of their terrestrial sisters, in particular the heaviness and darkness of Aysel Senguen— Ziad's German Turk, or Turkish German. Muhammad Atta had seen Aysel only once (bare legs, bare arms, bare hair), in the medical bookstore in Hamburg, and he had not forgotten her face. Ziad and Aysel were his control experiment for the life lived by sexual love; and for many months the two of them had peopled his insomnias. He knew that Aysel had come to Florida in January (and had scandalously accompanied Ziad to the flight school); he was also obscurely moved by the fact that a letter to her comprised Ziad's will and testament. And he kept wondering how their bodies conjoined, how she must open herself up to him, with all her heaviness and darkness . . . Muhammad Atta had decided that romantic and religious ardor came from contiguous parts of the human being: the parts he didn't have. Yet Ziad, as the obliterator of "law" (and the obliterator of United 93), was duly poised for mass murder. Only *roughly* contiguous, then: Ziad could say he was doing it for God, and many would believe him, but he couldn't say he was doing it for love. He wasn't doing it for love, or for God. He was doing it for the core reason, just like Muhammad Atta.

"All is well at Newark International?"

"All is well. We're in the sterile area. Did you see your precious imam?"

"I did. And he gave me the water."

"The water? What water?"

"The holy water," said Muhammad Atta, with delectation, "from the Oasis."

There was a silence. "What does it do?" said Ziad.

"It absolves you of what the imam called the 'enormity,' the atrocious crime, Ziad, of the self-felony."

There was another silence. But that was no longer true. Muhammad Atta thought he might be getting more out of this conversation if there hadn't been a mechanized floor-sweeper, resembling a hovercraft, with an old man on it, beeping and sniveling around his chair.

"I'm preparing to drink the holy water even as I speak."

"Does it come in a special bottle?"

"A crystal vial. God said, 'All those who hate me love and court death.' You see, Ziad, you are the trustee of your body, not its owner. God is its owner."

"And the water?"

"The water is within you and preserves you for God. It's a new technique—it began in Palestine. Your hell, Ziad, will burn with jet fuel for eternity. And eternity never ends—it never even begins. So there may be some delay before you get those brides of light. Perhaps you should have settled for your German nudist. Goodbye, Ziad."

He hung up, redialed, and had a more or less identical conversation with Marwan, minus the theme of Aysel. In the case of Marwan (the other half of "architecture," and just across the way, now, at United), different considerations obtained. The emphasis of their rivalry was not jihadi ardor so much as nihilistic insouciance. So the two of them exchanged yawning boasts, in code, about how low down, and at what angle, they would strike, and casually agreed that, if there were F-16s over New York, they would crash their planes into the streets . . . Finally, dutifully, he called Hani ("arts"), the only Saudi pilot, with whom he shared no history, and not much hatred. Muhammad Atta hoped that he hadn't decisively undermined Ziad, who, after all, was a Saudi short (or two Saudis short, if you discounted the punk-like Ahmed). No. He believed that he could safely rely, at this point, on the fierce physics of the peer group.

A peer group piously competitive about suicide, he had concluded, was a very powerful thing, and the West had no equivalent to it. A peer group for whom death was not death—and life was not life, either. Yet an inversion so extreme, he thought, would quickly become decadent: synagogues, nightclubs, nurseries, sunset homes. Transgression, by its nature, was helter-skelter: it had no choice but to escalate. And the thing would start to be over in a generation, as everyone slowly and incredulously intuited it: the core reason.

Perhaps the closest equivalent, or analogy, the West could field was the firefighters. Muhammad Atta had studied architecture and engineering. The fire that would be created by 20,000 gallons of jet fuel, he knew, could not be fought: the steel frame of the tower would buckle; the walls, which were not intended to be weight-bearing, would collapse, one onto the other; and down it would all come. The fire could not be fought, but there would be firefighters. They were called the "bravest," accurately, in his view; and, as the bravest, they took on a certain responsibility. The firefighters were saying, every day: "Who's going to do it, if we don't? If the bravest don't, who else is going to risk death to save the lives of strangers?"

As he sat for another few moments on the tin chair, as he watched the mall awaken and come into commercial being, filling up now with Americans and American purpose and automatic self-belief, he felt he had timed it about right. (And his face had timed it about right.) Because he couldn't possibly survive another day of the all-inclusive detestation—of the pan-anathema. This feeling had been his familiar since the age of twelve or thirteen; it had come upon him, like an illness without a symptom. Cairo, Hamburg, even the lemon-blue winter dawn over Kandahar: they had all looked the same to him. Unreal mockery.

Muhammad Atta took the bottle from his carry-on. The imam *said* it was from Medina. He shrugged, and drank the holy Volvic.

. . .

Boarding began with first class. And if Muhammad Atta ever found anything funny, he might have smiled at this: Wail and Waleed, the brothers, the two semi-literate yokels from the badlands of the Yemeni border, shuffling off to their thrones—2A and 2B. Then business. He led. Abdulaziz and Satam followed.

He hadn't even reached his seat when it hit him. It came with great purity of address, replacing everything else in his stretched sensorium. Even his headache, while not actually taking its leave, immediately stepped aside, almost with a flourish, to accommodate the new guest. It was a feeling that had abandoned him forever, he thought, four months ago—but now it was back. With twinkly promptitude, canned music flooded forth: a standard ballad, a flowery flute with many trills and graces. The breathy refrain joined the simmer of the engines; yet neither could drown the popping, the groaning, the creaking, as of a dungeon door to an inner sanctum—the ungainsayable anger of his bowels.

So now he sat gripping the armrests of 8D as the coach passengers filed by. Why did there have to be so *many* of them, always another briefcase, another backpack, always another buzzcut, another whitehair? . . . He waited, rose, and with grueling nonchalance, his buttocks clenched, sauntered forward. All three toilets claimed to be occupied. They were not occupied, he knew. A frequent and inquisitive traveler on American commercial jets, Muhammad Atta knew that the toilets were locked, like all the other toilets (this was the practice on tight turnarounds), and would remain locked until the plane leveled out. He pressed a flat hand against all three: again, the misery of recurrence, of duplication. He tried, but he couldn't abstain from a brief flurry of shoving and kicking and rattling. As he returned to 8D he saw that Abdulaziz was looking at him, not with commiseration, now, but with puzzled disappointment, even turning in his seat to exchange a responsible frown with Satam.

Strapped in, Muhammad Atta managed the following series of thoughts. You *needed* the belief system, the ideology, the ardor. You had to have it. The core reason was good enough for the mind. But it couldn't carry the body.

To the others, he realized, he was giving a detailed impersonation of a man who had lost his nerve. And he had not lost his nerve. Even before the plane gave its preliminary jolt (like a polite cough of introduction), he felt the pull of it, with relief, with recognition: the necessary speed, the escape velocity he needed to deliver him to his journey's end.

American 11 pushed back from Gate 32, Terminal B, at 7:40. There was the captain and the first officer; there were nine flight attendants, and seventy-six passengers, excluding Wail, Waleed, Satam, Abdulaziz, and Muhammad Atta. American 11 was in the air at 7:59.

Now he obliged himself to do what he had always intended to do, during the climb. He had a memory ready, and a thought experiment. He wanted to prepare himself for the opening of female flesh; he wanted to prepare himself for what would soon be happening to the throat of the stewardess—whom he could see, on her jump seat, head bowed low, with a pen in her hand and a clipboard on her lap.

In 1999 his return ticket from Afghanistan had put him on an Iberia flight from the U.A.E. to Madrid. They had just leveled out when he became aware of an altercation in the back of the plane. Swiveling in his seat, he saw that perhaps fifteen or sixteen men, turbaned and white-robed, had crowded into the aisle and were now on the floor, humped in prayer. You could hear the male flight attendant's monotonous and defeated remonstrations as he backed away. *"Por favor, señores. Es ilegal. Señores, por favor!"* Minutes later the captain came on the PA, saying in Spanish, English, and Gulf Arabic that if the passengers didn't return to their seats he would most certainly return to Dubai. Then she appeared. Even Muhammad Atta at once conceded that here was the dark female in her most swinishly luxurious form: tall, long-necked, herself streamlined and aerodynamic, with hair like a billboard for a chocolate sundae, and all that flesh, damp and glowing as if from fever or lust. She came to a halt and gave a roll of the eyes that took her whole head with it; then she surged forward with great scooping motions of her hands, bellowing—*"Vamos arriba, coños!"* And the kneeling men had to peer out at this seraph of breast and haunch and uniformed power, and straighten up and scowl, and slowly grope for their seats. Muhammad Atta had felt only contempt for the men crooked over the patterned carpet; but he would never forget the face of the stewardess—the face of cloudless entitlement—and how badly he had wanted to hurt it.

And yet—no, it wasn't going to work. For him, the combination, up close, was wholly unmanageable: the combination of women and blood. So far, he thought, this is the worst day of my life—provably the worst day. In his head the weary fight between the vermin was finished; one was dying, and was now being disgustingly eaten by the other. And his loins, between them, were contriving for him something very close to the sensations of anal rape. So far, this was the worst day of his life. But then every day was the worst day, because every day was the most recent day, and the most developed, the most advanced (with all those other days behind it) toward the pan-anathema.

The plane was flattening out. He waited for the order. This would be given by the captain, when he turned off the fasten-seat-belts sign.

We have some planes, said Muhammad Atta, coolly. *Just stay quiet, and you'll be okay. We are returning to the airport. Nobody move. Everything will be okay. If you try to make any moves, you'll endanger yourself and the airplane. Just stay quiet.*

He had stepped through the region of inexpressible sordor, and gained the cockpit. Here, in the grotto of the mad clocksmith, was more cringing flesh and more blood—but manageably male. Now he disengaged the computer and prepared to fly by direct law.

It was 8:24. He laughed for the first time since childhood: he was in the Atlantic of the sky, at the controls of the biggest weapon in history.

At 8:27 he made a grand counter-clockwise semicircle, turning south.

At 8:44 he began his descent.

The core reason was of course all the killing—all the putting to death. Not the crew, not the passengers, not the office workers in the Twin Towers, not the cleaners and the caterers, not the men of the NYPD and the FDNY. He was thinking of the war, the wars, the war-cycles that would flow from this day. He didn't believe in the Devil, as an active force, but he did believe in death. Death, at certain times, stopped moving at its even pace and broke into a hungry, lumbering run. Here was the primordial secret. No longer closely guarded— no longer well kept. Killing was divine delight. And your suicide was just a part of the contribution you made—the massive contribution to death. All your frigidities and futilities were rewritten, becoming swollen with meaning. This was what was possible when you turned the tides of life around, when you ran with the beasts, when you flew with the flies.

First, the lesser totems of Queens, like a line of defense for the tutelary godlings of the island.

When he came clattering in over the struts and slats of Manhattan, there it was ahead of him and below him—the thing which is called World. Cross streets, blocks, districts, shot out from underneath the speedlines of the plane. He was glad that he wouldn't have to plow down into the city, and he even felt love for it, all its strivings and couplings and sunderings. And he felt no impulse to increase power or to bank or to strike even lower. It was reeling him in. Now even the need to shit felt right and good as his destination surged toward him.

· · ·

There are many accounts, uniformly incomplete, of what it is like to die slowly. But there is no information at all about what it is like to die suddenly and violently. We are being gentle when we describe such deaths as *instant*. "The passengers died instantly." Did they? It may be that some people can do it, can die instantly. The very old, because the vital powers are weak; the very young, because there is no great accretion of experience needing to be scattered. Muhammad Atta was thirty-three. As for him (and perhaps this is true even in cases of vaporization; perhaps this was true even for the wall shadows of Japan), it took much longer than an instant. By the time the last second arrived, the first second seemed as far away as childhood.

American 11 struck at 8:46:40. Muhammad Atta's body was beyond all healing by 8:46:41; but his mind, his presence, needed time to shut itself down. The physical torment—a panic attack in every nerve, a riot of the atoms—merely italicized the last shinings of his brain. They weren't thoughts; they were more like a series of unignorable conclusions, imposed from without. Here was the hereafter, after all; and here was the reckoning. His mind groaned and fumbled with an irreconcilability, a defeat, a self-cancellation. Could he assemble the argument? It follows—by definition—if and only if . . .

And then the argument assembled all by itself. The joy of killing was proportional to the value of what was destroyed. But that value was something a killer could never see and never gauge. And where was the joy he thought he had felt—where *was* that joy, that itch, that paltry tingle? Yes, how gravely he had underestimated it. How very gravely he had underestimated life. His own he had hated, and had wished away; but see how long it was taking to absent itself—and with what helpless grief was he watching it go, imperturbable in its beauty and its power. Even as his flesh fried and his blood boiled, there was life, kissing its finger-tips. Then it echoed out, and ended.

2

On September 11, 2001, he opened his eyes at 4 a.m., in Port-land, Maine; and Muhammad Atta's last day began.

APRIL 2006. *The New Yorker*

Iran and the Lord of Time

The American politician whom Mahmoud Ahmadinejad most closely resembles—in one crucial respect—is Ronald Reagan. General similarities, I agree, are hard to spot. Ahmadinejad doesn't live on a ranch with a former starlet. As a young Republican, Reagan wasn't involved in the murder of prominent Democrats. Ahmadinejad doesn't use Grecian 2000. Reagan didn't have a degree in traffic control. And so on. But what they have in common is this: both men are denizens of that stormlit plain where end-time theology meets nuclear weapons.

Now we can return, for a while, to dissimilarities. Ahmadinejad is not checked and balanced by democratic institutions. Reagan did not actually spend public money on civic preparations for the Second Coming. Ahmadinejad does not have a temperament in which "simple-minded idealism" (this is Eric Hobsbawm's account of the breakthrough with Gorbachev in Reykjavik) might break through the dense screen of "careerists, desperadoes and professional warriors around him" and recognize "the sinister absurdity" of the arms race. Reagan was not the product of a culture saturated in dreams of morbid torment, self-mutilation, and mass martyrdom. Finally, whereas Reagan had enough firepower to kill everybody on earth at least once over, Ahmadinejad does not yet have his bomb.

Jesus Christ, according to both men, is due very shortly, but in Ahmadinejad's vision Christ will merely be part of the entourage of a much grander personage — the Hidden Imam. Who is the Hidden Imam? In the year 873, the bloodline of the Prophet came to an end when Hasan al-Askari (in Shiism the eleventh legitimate imam) died without an heir. At that point, among the believers, a classic circularity took hold. It was assumed that Hasan *must* have an heir; there was no record of his existence, they reasoned, because extraordinary efforts had been made to conceal it; and extraordinary efforts had been made because this son was an extraordinary imam — the Mahdi, in fact, or the Lord of Time.

In Shia eschatology the Mahdi returns during a period of great tribulation (during a nuclear war, for instance), delivers the faithful from injustice and oppression, and supervises the Day of Judgement. When that happens, the Muslims have won: the Shia have won. Not only Ahmadinejad but members of his cabinet are now giving the Hidden Imam "about four years" — in other words, within the current presidential term. And where has the Hidden Imam dwelt since the ninth century? In "occultation," wherever that may be, as he counts off the days till his reappearance. Rightly is he called the Lord of Time: he is more than eleven hundred years old.

Before we come to all the other reasons for not allowing Iran, under any circumstances, to develop nuclear weapons, let us take a brief, surrealistic look at the Iranian identity,

which has two poles: Cyrus the Great and Muhammad,
Persepolis and Qom—the imperially sensuous and the imperially pious. In 1935 Iranians found themselves living in a
different country—not Persia but Iran, the specifically pre-
Islamic "land of the Arians." This was the work of the secu-
larizer Reza Shah, Iran's Atatürk or Nasser. In 1976 Iranians
found themselves living in a different millennium—not
1355 (dated from the time of Muhammad), but 2535 (dated
from the birth of Cyrus the Great). This was the work of
Reza Shah's son. Then came the Revolution. It is now called
the Islamic Revolution, but it was not an Islamic revolution.
It became Islamic when it was over, because the mullahs had
a near-monopoly of violence, and could also field the charismatic glower of the Ayatollah Khomeini.

After 1979, Iran was subjected to militant and breakneck
re-Islamization. Pre-Muhammadan times were declared to
be *jahiliyyah,* a benighted toilet of ignorance and idolatry,
and a dire embarrassment to all good Muslims. In the mid-
1990s, for example, the historian Jahangir Tafazoli was murdered simply because he was the best-known expert on
ancient Iran. But you will recognize the indivisibility of the
sensual and the pious in the Iranian character when I tell you
that the author of this quietly beautiful quatrain—

> I am a supplicant for a goblet of wine
> from the hand of a sweetheart.
> In whom can I confide this secret of mine,
> Where can I take this sorrow?

—is the Ayatollah Khomeini. As against that, to come full
circle, this was the fate of Khomeini's father: himself an aya-

tollah, Khomeini Sr. was murdered by a friend of a man who had been sentenced to death, by Khomeini Sr., for eating in daylight during Ramadan.

Mystical, volatile, and masochistic, and so violent that a protest about bus fares can leave thirty dead, Iranians, one might cautiously suggest, are not yet ready for the force that drives the sun. Everyone knows what Ahmadinejad thinks of Israel (and we remember his Islamists' conference, or his goons' rodeo, in Tehran, on the historicity of the Holocaust). This is what Rafsanjani thinks of Israel—Rafsanjani, the old, much-jailed revolutionary chancer, a pragmatist and reformer, hugely worldly, hugely corrupt: "the use of even one nuclear bomb inside Israel will destroy everything," whereas a counterstrike on Iran will merely "harm" the Islamic world. "It is not irrational to contemplate such an eventuality."

At first the calculation seems to resemble that of the Hindu fundamentalists who advocated nuclear war with Pakistan. And yet it is not just a question of weight of numbers. A better analogy would be with Bolshevism in its strictly Leninist phase: ideology is placed over nation. Iranians call the Iran–Iraq War (1980–88) "the Imposed War." In fact it was the Provoked War, which then became the Self-Perpetuating War, because Khomeini made it a test of Islam, with pan-Shiism as the stated goal. And it was for this that the little martyrs filed through the minefields and then sprinted into the machine-gun fire. In the West, we're all supposed to feel terrible about having supported Saddam (allowing him to avoid outright defeat). But the far greater danger was an expansionist and triumphalist Khomeini.

Rule number one: no theocracy can be allowed to wield a nuclear weapon. For the Iranians, as an Israeli official put it, Mutual Assured Destruction "is not a deterrent. It's an incentive." Indeed, the more you look into it, the more you wonder why we are having an illegitimate fiasco in Iraq when we could be having a legitimate fiasco in Iran. Yes, where *was* the President's spell-check tsar? With Iran, we have a cornucopia of casus belli: strong links with al-Qaeda; known facilitation of September 11; and twenty years of vigorous nuclear weaponization, an epic of ring magnets and milling machines, of calutrons and cyclotrons, assisted by practically every country on earth except Israel. And there are dozens of others, like the unavenged U.S. marines of Beirut. With Iran, too, we have a population that is strongly if ambivalently pro-American. To the youth of Iran (a large majority), *America* is the Mahdi—the redeemer, the Lord of Time.

Nuclear weapons, it seems, were sent down here to provide mankind with a succession of unbearable dilemmas. And we should say at this point that the West's anti-proliferation policy is a moral and philosophical non-starter. When the Administration talks of depriving Iran of nuclear weapons by means of (new-generation) nuclear weapons, we may wonder how convincing this will sound to a country whose core dread is invasion (they have suffered it from the Greeks, the Parthians, the Arabs, the Mongols, the Afghans, the Turks, the Russians, and the British) and whose core value is universal equality and justice.

The solution is both entirely obvious and entirely unattainable. We must give the Iranians some face; and then all seven nuclear powers must begin to scale back toward the zero option; and the Middle East must be declared a nuclear-free zone. Many Israeli patriots now wish that the Jewish state had been established, not in Palestine, but in, say, Bavaria. Who would worry about a few leather-shorted scoutmasters from the BLO? As it is, Israel has Ahmadinejad to worry about. He may delegate First Use to Hezbollah or, perhaps, to the Call of Islam or the Legion of the Pure. Or he may himself choose to become the first suicide-bomber to be measured in megatons.

JUNE 2006. The New York Times Syndicate

What Will Survive of Us

A t 8:21 the first plane, American 11, turned off its
transponder (the automatic tracking device); then it
changed course and began its descent. The air traffic controllers were still trying to locate American 11 when word
came through that "a light plane" had hit the World Trade
Center (at 8:46). On CNN they saw the scene of the crash.
The wound in the building's side was in the shape of a plane;
and they knew at once that it wasn't a Cessna or a twin-
prop. It was what they call a "heavy"—a wide-body commercial jet.

In the real-time docudrama *United 93,* we see the second
plane strike its target, not on CNN, but, so to speak, with the
naked eye. What appears to be the original footage, star-
tlingly, has been placed within a vast vista of morning blue.
Our POV is the glass-skinned control post at Newark International. By now the North Tower, to the right, is like a

Review of *United 93,* directed by Paul Greengrass (Universal Pictures,
2006)

demonic smokestack, giving off a leaning column of furry black fumes. As the second plane (United 175) impends, the controllers gasp at its velocity. Muhammad Atta's incision, in the North Tower, will now look surgically discreet—compared to the kinetic ecstasy sought by Marwan al-Shehhi. United 175 was traveling at nearly 600 mph, a speed that the 767 was not designed to reach, let alone sustain. This happened eleven seconds and three minutes after nine o'clock—the core moment of September 11. Now they knew; and so, about thirty minutes later, did the passengers on United 93.

That plane, too, was traveling at 580 mph when it crashed, nose first and upside down, forming a crater 175 feet deep in an empty field near Shanksville, Pennsylvania. Of the three thousand who died on that day, only those on board the fourth plane had no doubts about the fate intended for them. The director of *United 93,* Paul Greengrass, is right: they were "the first people to inhabit the post-9/11 world." We may strongly identify with one passenger, an earnest Scandinavian, who cannot accept the new reality: he argues for full cooperation with the hijackers, hoping, one assumes, for a leisurely siege on some sweltering North African tarmac. The others know, from cellphones and airphones, that it isn't going to be like that. They rise up, and the plane comes down. United 93 took off at 8:42; the hijack began at 9:28; the passengers and crew started making their calls at about 9:35; the revolt was launched at 9:57; United 93 hit the ground at 10:03:11—one hour (to the second) after the crash of United 175.

As the film nears its conclusion you will find yourself, I am confident, in a state of near-perfect distress—a distress that knows no blindspots. The *New York Times* called *United 93* "the feel-bad movie of the year." This description is trivial. The distress is something you can taste, like a cud, returned from the stomach for further mastication: the ancient flavor of death and defeat. You think: this is exactly what they meant us to feel. And your mind will cast about for some-thing, a molecule, an atom of consolation; and what you will reach for is what the passengers reached for.

Those that go through mortal fear also experience a fierce adoration of life—just as the prisoner on death row finds water delicious, finds air delicious. And before battle a sol-dier's heart is said to be full of love. This somber, end-time love is not usually articulated; its articulation, on the planes of September 11, was made possible by that gigantic contrib-utor to our daily reality, the mobile phone. Like the victims on the other three planes, but unlike them (because they knew that many, many hundreds of their compatriots had already died on that morning), the passengers called their families and said that they loved them. In retrospect it feels like an extraordinary validation, or fulfillment, of Larkin's lines at the end of "An Arundel Tomb" (1956):

> . . . to prove
> Our almost-instinct almost true:
> What will survive of us is love.

A Hollywoodized version of the story would begin with Bruce Willis, in the part of Todd Beamer ("Let's roll"), waking in Manhattan, and languidly reminding his wife that he is off to San Francisco on an early flight from Newark. *United 93* begins with the desolate, self-hypnotizing drone of early-morning prayer. In their budget hotel room the four hijackers, wearing clean white vests, are aspiring to the murderous serenity urged on them by their handlers in Afghanistan. Soon they are among the passengers and are being processed to the gate. We are in the familiar, and suddenly painful, everyday: the spotty young woman with her laptop; the shared travel anxiety of an elderly couple; the grunt of relief from a panting young man, pleased, as you would be, to get there just in time. And it is here, in the departure bay, that Greengrass makes his one major divergence from the known: Ziad Jarrah, the pilot and leader (and in all senses a different breed from the muscle Saudis), says six words into his mobile phone—"I love you. I love you."

Greengrass may have other sources. According to a footnote in *The 9/11 Commission Report,* Jarrah did make a final call to his fiancée, Aysel Senguen; but he called her from the hotel, and she described their conversation as brief and not unusual. Thus the moment in the departure bay, though broadly justifiable, is hugely anomalous, and for this reason: it is artistic. And elsewhere, while Greengrass cannot banish his talents of eye and ear, he refuses the artistic, and quite rightly. Those six words hang in the air, and are balanced and answered by the tearful protestations of the doomed passengers. In this reading, Jarrah, too, knew what would survive of him.

What is not in doubt is that Jarrah loved Aysel Senguen. He is, by many magnitudes, the least repulsive of the nineteen killers of September 11. An affluent Lebanese, he left the beaches and discos of Beirut at the age of twenty-one, in 1996, and went to Germany to study dentistry (he later switched to aeronautics). There he met and fell in love with Aysel Senguen, the student daughter of a Turkish immigrant. He was human in other ways. Defying cadre policy, he stayed close to his family, and made several returns to the bedside of his ailing father in Lebanon. Most centrally, he had doubts, and needed to be cajoled and rallied right to the end. And all this is there in the extraordinary performance of Khalid Abdalla. There are no weak points, and no obtrusively strong points, in the *United 93* ensemble. But among the little-knowns and the unknowns and the people playing themselves, Abdalla, perhaps destabilizingly for the movie, is something like its star. His history is all held in, yet it is all there in his suffering eyes.

At Newark International there was a routine—indeed wholly predictable—delay on the ground, caused by weight of traffic. It is likely that those twenty-five minutes changed everything. If United had left on time, the chances are that there would have been no passenger revolt. Instead, there would have been horror at the White House or horror at the Capitol. Osama bin Laden wanted the White House; Muhammad Atta, the operational leader, vaguely argued that the approach to Pennsylvania Avenue would be too difficult, and wanted the Capitol. Interestingly, the President was not in the White House (he was puzzling his way through "The Pet Goat" in Sarasota, Florida), but the President's wife might well have been in the Capitol (pushing No Child Left Behind). In any case, both buildings were being evacuated by 9:30—two minutes after the hijack of United 93.

Greengrass peels off, at punctual intervals, to follow the

traffic controllers (whose efforts were impressive) and to follow the military (whose efforts were pitiable); but by now
the other three planes have crashed, and the focus is all on
United 93. Sickening suspense about the revolt of the terrorists is replaced, hereafter, by sickening suspense about the
revolt of the passengers. In the aftermath of that day, a CIA
official tastefully noted that—even though the government
spent $40 billion a year on internal security—all that stood
between America and September 11 was "a bunch of rugby
players." But America didn't even have that. On United 93
there is no bunch, no pack, of rugby players. There is one
huge athlete who spearheads the charge (with a marvelously
giddy, drunken expression on his face); but he leads a motley
band—they are just passengers, after all. The looming coun-
tercoup is rendered in strict accordance with Greengrass's
method. There is no final powwow, there are no husky vale-
dictions. It simply erupts, with desperate suddenness, and
they are coming down the aisle with their weapons—
kitchen knives, wine bottles, boiling water.

And they didn't really have a chance. This was one of the
existential nightmares of United 93. They were up in the sky
at maximum throttle in a huge machine. But no one on board
knew how to land it. Not Jarrah, who was trained only for
level flight. By now the passengers are using the drinks cart as
a battering-ram, and Jarrah, lover of Aysel Senguen, is doing
what he can to make the plane yaw, then pitch, then dive.
These are the last words on the black box, translated from the
Arabic, each and every one of them utterly futile, and utterly
meaningless: "Allah is the greatest! Allah is the greatest! Is
that it? I mean, shall we put it down?" "Yes, put it in it, and

pull it down." We can say, at least, that the passengers saved America from a fourth scar on its psyche. And there is that glimmer of double meaning in the film's title. And that is all.

Greengrass doesn't spare us—but he spares us something. When was the last time you boarded an airplane that had no children in it? *United 93* has no children in it. It is hard to defend your imagination from such a reality (and the Internet will not willingly tell you about the children on the planes of September 11). "What's happening? Well, you see, my child, the men with the bloodstained knives think that if they kill themselves, and all of us, we will stop trying to destroy Islam and they will go at once to a paradise of women and wine." No, I suppose you would just tell him or her that you loved them, and he or she would tell you that they loved you too. Love is an abstract noun, something nebulous. And yet love turns out to be the only part of us that is solid, as the world turns upside down and the screen goes black. We can't tell if it will survive us. But we can be sure that it's the last thing to go.

JUNE 2006. *The Times*

Conspiracy Theories, and *Takfir*

"T"he *Frankfurter Zeitung* repeats again and again that the *Protocols* are [*sic*] forgeries," wrote Adolf Hitler in *Mein Kampf* (1924). He meant *The Protocols of the Elders of Zion,* which purported to be the minutes of a conference held by a coven of power-crazed old Jews, and was in fact the inflammatory concoction of the Okhrana, or the tsarist secret police. "This alone," Hitler went on, with a little cluck of satisfaction, "is evidence of their authenticity."

Readers should now prepare themselves for an orgy of credulousness. Asked in a recent survey to explain their presence in Iraq, 85 percent of American soldiers said that the "main mission" was "to retaliate for Saddam's role" in the September attacks. About two-thirds of American civilians, it's true, share that misapprehension; but it is implausible that front-line troops are so incuriously risking their lives. This near-consensus on the question cannot be due to ignorance.

Review of *The Looming Tower: Al-Qaeda and the Road to 9/11* by Lawrence Wright (Alfred A. Knopf, 2006)

It comes from the same wishfulness that fortifies the majority belief, among Muslims, that September 11 was the work of Mossad (and that July 7, 2005, was the work of the French—incensed by losing out to Britain in their bid for the Olympics).

Although few Americans think the Israelis were responsible for September 11, nearly half of them (42 percent) think the *Americans* did it. This means that the average American is slightly more distrustful of the U.S. government than the average Pakistani (in Pakistan a mere 41 percent consider that the attacks were not carried out by Islamic terrorists—as against 59 percent of Turks and Egyptians and 65 percent of Indonesians). American "skeptics" hold that the collapse of the Twin Towers was caused by expert demolition. They hold that the explosion at the Pentagon was consistent, not with a crashed 767, but with a cruise missile. In other words, Washington wounded itself.

It is of course miserably predictable that there is, in the U.K., a thriving counter-theory about July 7. My pen grows heavy in my hand (and I begin to weary of the sun), but here it is: in order to "distract" the "public" from its other "crimes," the "government" committed four massacres on that day, and "blamed" them on Islam. The July 7 pipe-dreamers, at their meetings and rallies, take a violent tone, and are quick to issue death threats to their opponents in blogsville; but on the front where terror and boredom march in step, the illusionists' first loyalty is to tedium. "We just want you to weigh the evidence," they say. In other words, they just want you to sit still and listen to an epic of futile pedantry. The bores, and the terrorists, are alike confessing to impotence. If realpolitik is all smoke and mirrors and supercynicism, then why not embrace marginality, and exclude yourself from the political and the real?

Psychiatrists call it fabulation. The rest of us call it the conspiracy theory—or the masochistic lust for chicanery and compound deceit. Fabulation may more simply be the failure to assimilate; and we concede that September 11 will perhaps never be wholly assimilable. The first question to be asked of the fabulist is *cui bono?* And the answer would be, "Well, the Administration, which could then accrue the power . . . to march on Baghdad." We are arriving at an axiom in long-term thinking about international terrorism: the real danger lies, not in what it inflicts, but in what it provokes. Thus by far the gravest consequence of September 11, to date, is Iraq.

The American death toll in the war will soon exceed the death toll in the original assault; and for the Iraqi people, now, that figure is exceeded every three weeks. Nor are the losses merely actuarial: they are also to be seen in our enfeebled hold on the high ground of morality and reason. It is as if September 11 brought about a net increase in suggestibility, and at every level. At the top, a president who assigns himself the unusually bold project of "remaking" the Middle East, and thus the world; at the bottom, a citizenry haunted by rudderlessly cruising suspicion. The fact is that America didn't wound itself in September 2001, as the fabulists claim. It did that in March 2003, and thereafter.

In *The Looming Tower: Al-Qaeda and the Road to 9/11,* Lawrence Wright's tough-minded and cussedly persistent narrative opens with portraits of the grand triumvirate of developed Islamism: Sayyid Qutb, Ayman al-Zawahiri, and Osama bin Laden. And almost at once the question arises: Should we be solaced, or additionally galled, by the poverty of the human material now so ferociously ranged against us? In these pages we meet some formidable schemers and killers, like Khaled Sheikh Muhammad, the author of "the Planes Operation" (and since imprisoned). As for the other players, there are nuances, there are shades of black; but the consistent profile is marked by intellectual vacuity, by a fanaticism that simply thirsts for the longest possible penal code, and, most basically, by a chaotically adolescent—or even juvenile—indifference to reality. These men are fabulists crazed with blood and death; and reality, for them, is just something you have to maneuver around in order to destroy it.

Qutb (1906−66), an Egyptian writer and civil servant, does duty as the first framer of Islamism. And you wonder about the condition of the Muslim imagination, so easily "captured" by this almost endearingly comical blunderer. His fate, at the hands of Nasser, was not at all comical; and Qutb's martyrdom was his controlled historical time bomb. Islamism, at any rate, owes to him the twin dreams of planetary domination and theocratic genocide. Zawahiri, Qutb's compatriot, gives further weight to the argument that what they call IT (international terrorism) was born and raised in the prisons of Cairo. Torture is always the first recourse of a terrorized state (even Ted Heath reached for it early on in the Troubles). And in a sense terrorism is a gamble on torture. Will torture deter—or will it further radicalize? It further radicalized Zawahiri.

Originally a medical man, Zawahiri became the leader and moral tutor of his own chapter of Islamism, al-Jihad, where he deployed the doctrine or heresy (or tinkertoy sophistry) of *takfir*. As Wright deftly explains,

> The takfiris convinced themselves that salvation for all of humanity lay on the other side of moral territory that had always been the certain province of the damned. They would shoulder the risks to their eternal souls by assuming the divine authority of deciding who was a real Muslim and who was not, who should live and who should die.

This greatly expanded the population of the killable. Indeed, no martialized doctrine in history has availed itself of a vaster target—absolutely anyone at all. *Takfir* was an ancient and recurrent notion in Islam, and Zawahiri resurrected it. Bin Laden, as usual, just fell into line.

"Unfortunately," said one of Osama's companions, "his IQ was not that great." And this verdict stands. In a 1997 interview on CNN, Osama was asked about the kind of society he envisaged for Saudi Arabia. This was the point-by-point program he had in mind:

> We are confident, with the permission of God, praise and glory be to Him, that Muslims will be victorious in the Arabian Peninsula and that God's religion, praise and glory be to Him, will prevail in the peninsula [sharia law already prevailed in the peninsula]. It is a great pride and a big hope that the revelation unto

Muhammad, peace be upon him, will be resorted to for ruling. When we used to follow Muhammad's revelation, peace be upon him, we were in great happiness and in great dignity, to God belongs the credit and praise.

Bin Laden's contribution is his image, and nothing more: omnicidal nullity under a halo of ascetic beatitude. His personal deformation remains mysterious. Zawahiri was jailed and tortured. Qutb was jailed, tortured, and executed. Nobody traumatized bin Laden; unlike his mentors, he was not internally rewired by the whips and the electric cables. Almost alone among a shifting crew of mono-eyed mullahs, tin-legged zealots, blind sheikhs, and paralyzed clerics, bin Laden did at least have the wit to stay in one piece.

I found myself frivolously wondering whether Osama was just the product of his family background—and more particularly of his birth order. Seventeenth out of fifty-seven is a notoriously difficult slot to fill; and if the polygamous father is also an illiterate billionaire, then an appetite for conflict, among his older sons, should not surprise us. In fact, Osama's vehemence is cultivated, worked-up. This is from a manifesto of 1989:

What is required is to wage an economic war against America. We have to boycott all American products . . . They're taking the money we pay them for their products and giving it to the Jews to kill our brothers.

"Any American we see," he concluded, in words that drip and seethe with menace, "we should notify of our complaints.

We should write to American embassies." *Write to* American embassies? His position was to harden—all the way to *takfir*.

At the time of his Declaration of War against America (1996), bin Laden was moldering away in a cave in Tora Bora—stateless, penniless, and half-starved. His achievements were a matter of myth, of fabulation; he was a funk-ridden and incompetent ex-jihadi (a mere pepperer of the Red Army); and he was a serial business flop. In short, he was a terrorist financier who had run out of cash; and he was now entirely at the mercy of the local Islamist power, the village-idiot vigilantes known as the Taliban. Very soon, Zawahiri would be in a Russian jail, and bin Laden would be subsisting on stale bread and contaminated water. At this stage al-Qaeda's survival looked unlikely; and its chances of mounting an operation the size of September 11 were infinitesimal. The "declaration," then, was little more than a deathbed whimper.

How, then, did the cornered troglodyte of 1996 become the radiant Mahdi of 2001? Bin Laden's fame was lucrative: in 1998 the Taliban leader, Mullah Omar, started taking bribes from Riyadh as a down payment for Osama's extradition and delivery to the Americans. But Omar and Osama were soulmates—and business partners. That same summer saw the bombing of the American embassies in Kenya and Tanzania. In Nairobi, al-Qaeda killed 206 Africans and wounded 4,500 (150 were blinded by flying glass); it also killed a total of twelve Americans; the half-bungled attack in Dar es Salaam killed no Americans at all. Although the Islamic reaction, worldwide, was one of near-unanimous disgust, it was, definingly, the American reaction that empowered bin Laden.

Of the sixty-six U.S. cruise missiles fired at the camps around Khost, in Afghanistan, a certain number failed to detonate. According to Wright (his source is Russian intelligence), "bin Laden sold the unexploded missiles to China for $10 million." In al-Qaeda's next attack, on the USS *Cole* in 2000, the symbolism was rather more finely tuned: a futuristic fighting ship crippled by a dinghy. Established as the global champion of the anti-American cause, bin Laden was now the recipient of fresh recruits bearing Samsonite suitcases stuffed with petrodollars from awed admirers in the Gulf.

September 11 itself emerges as a chapter of hideous coincidences. In its early days the Planes Operation consisted of two monoglot "muscle" Saudis blundering around Los Angeles—incapable, it seemed, of asking the way to the nearest flight school. All was set fair for yet another of al-Qaeda's ridiculous failures, on a par, perhaps, with the plan to assassinate the Pope (abandoned soon after the purchase of the killers' cassocks). The spectacular assault, "the big one," was a non-starter until the fortuitous arrival, in Kandahar, of the "Hamburg contingent" (Atta et al.): these men were superficially Westernized, and superficially rational; they were possessed by just the right kind of functioning insanity. Negative coincidences also characterized the American end of the story. It is painful to follow the inter-agency malfunctions, resentments, and pseudo-legalisms that opened the window to disaster. The man who came closest to averting it, John O'Neill, quit the FBI in the summer of 2001. He took up his new job on August 23: head of security at the World Trade Center. He had nineteen days to live.

Expert opinion, in the West, is now largely persuaded that al-Qaeda, as we knew it, is more or less finished. The "base"—justly so called in the adjectival sense—has become, we hear, "a state of mind." And what *is* that state of mind? One convinced that it is possible, simultaneously, to be a random mass murderer and a good Muslim. A death-brimmed bog of circular gullibility and paranoia, it is the state of mind of the weaponized fabulist. The conspiracy being detected here is the infidel campaign to obliterate the faith. It all began with the retreat of the Turkish armies from Vienna and the confirmation of Islamic decline. The year was 1683 and the day was September 11.

SEPTEMBER 2006. *The Times*

Bush in Yes-Man's-Land

George W. Bush has prevailed in two general elections because, very broadly, male voters feel that he's the kind of guy they "can have a beer with." Whereas in fact George W. Bush is the kind of guy they *can't* have a beer with, under any circumstances whatever: as they say at AA, he has come to treasure his sobriety. You can have a beer with John Kerry and Al Gore; and you can have a beer with Bush Sr. and Bill Clinton (and pretty well all the others, including George Washington). But you can't have a beer with Bush Jr.

Bush Sr.'s mucker and soulmate Brent Scowcroft was surprised by Bush Jr.'s ascendancy. "As best Scowcroft could calculate," writes Bob Woodward, "George W. Bush didn't know who he was until he was about forty-five. And now he was President?" Five years later, old Brent sadly contemplates Bush Sr., who is "anguished" and "tormented" by the Iraq War and its aftermath. "Condi is a disappointment, isn't

Review of *State of Denial: Bush at War, Part III* by Bob Woodward (Simon & Schuster, 2006)

she?" says Bush Sr. wanly (loath to blame his boy). "She's not up to the job." As for the other key players, Cheney seems unrecognizable ("It's a chorus. 'We don't know this Dick Cheney'"); and Rumsfeld dependably remains "a wholly negative force."

And what about the inner inner circle—Laura? Every six weeks she has a session with Andy Card (Chief of Staff, since resigned). "I can't talk about that," says Card, when pressed for more information on Iraq. "Well, he won't tell me either," says Laura. On weekends at Camp David, Laura takes long walks with Condi, so we may be sure she knows what's what. "He's happy with this," the First Lady tells Card, referring to the First Gentleman, "but I'm not. I don't know why he's not upset with this."

Is Bush "upset with this"? Or is he the only human being in the Western world who is "happy with this"? As I have already said, psychohistorians point to two internal mechanisms that allow us to live, for a while, with an unendurable truth: "numbing" (whereby the self is drained of affect), and also "doubling" (whereby the self divides into the ventricle that knows and the ventricle that doesn't). Bush isn't "doubling." What he seems to be doing is "bubbling": isolated from all discordant counsel, he has swaddled himself in "unshakeable conviction." The best reason for going into Iraq, in 2003, was to help bring about the healing of its people—a people often referred to in these pages as "an abused child," "a traumatized child." And what have we done to that child? As its new guardian, Bush can't not know what he has done to that child.

One of the many deranging consequences of September 11

was the reification of American power. Until that date, "U.S. hegemony" was largely a matter of facts and figures, of graphs and pie charts. Thereafter it became a matter of options and capabilities, of war plans cracked out on the President's desk. We can understand the afflatus, the rush of blood, in the White House: overnight, demonstrably, and palpably, a tax-cutting dry drunk from West Texas became the most powerful man in human history. One wonders, nowadays, how it goes with Bush, in his glands and his sinews. From September 11 to the autumn of 2003, he had the body language of the man in the bar who isn't going anywhere till he has had his fist fight. Now he looks washed, rinsed, bleached, his flat smile an awful rictus; that upper lip has lost all its lift.

Students of history are aware that illusion—or, if you prefer, psychopathology—plays a part in shaping world events. It is always a heavy call on human fortitude to acknowledge that such a thing is happening before our eyes, in broad daylight and full consciousness. On the opposing side we see illusion in its rawest form: virtuous and murderous fanaticism. On ours, we see a vertiginous power rush followed by a vacuum, and then a drift into helplessness and paralysis. That vacuum was itself reified after the fall of Baghdad, when the plunder began and the soldiers stood and watched, and it slowly emerged that *there was no policy for the peace*. Then came a dual disintegration, like that of the Twin Towers: the collapse of the authority of the state, and the collapse of the value of human life.

In his two previous books on the foreign policy of the current Administration, Woodward deployed his main journalistic strength—privileged access. *Bush at War* (Afghanistan) and *Plan of Attack* (the Iraq invasion) were the blushing beneficiaries of Washingtonian hubris, with all the key players queueing up to boast and crow. In *State of Denial,* Woodward slinks through a tight-mouthed pall of failure. He gets a couple of creepy afternoons with Rumsfeld, but now the information is coming his way at one remove, if not two. Should there be a further book, say in 2008, one fears that Woodward will be reduced to grilling the interns.

Still, we get a pretty fair idea of how it all happened. The dynamic was unanimity of belief: the establishment, by ideological filtration, of a yes-man's-land. Talented experts with dissenting views were sidelined: "Rumsfeld said that they needed people who were truly committed and who had not written or said things that were not supportive." And so on, system-wide, in an atmosphere of feuds and grudges, of tantrums and bollockings. In these pages, Powell, Rice, and Rumsfeld are seen to agree on only one proposition: that the U.S. government is fundamentally "dysfunctional." Otherwise, Woodward's only real bombshell is the following: "If we get somebody [an enemy combatant] and we can't get them to cooperate, we'll hand them over to you." That's Bush to Prince Bandar of Saudi Arabia on September 13, 2001.

Two misleadingly comical anecdotes reveal the abysmal depths of Coalition unpreparedness. Having allowed the dispersed Iraqi army to stay dispersed, the American viceroy started building a new one, catchily called the NIC (or New Iraqi Corps). It was pointed out, after a while, that this was the Arabic equivalent of calling it the FUQ. Similarly, when

Frank Miller of the National Security Council joined a Humvee patrol in Baghdad (March 2004), he was heartened to see that all the Iraqi children were giving him the thumbs-up sign, unaware that in Iraq the thumb (shorter yet chunkier) does duty for the middle digit.

But it may be that the Bush miscalculation was more chronological than geographical. In his sternly compelling book *The Shia Revival,* Vali Nasr suggests that the most momentous consequence of the Iraq adventure is the ignition of the Muslim fratricide, or sectarian war. Not the one between moderate and extreme Islam, which is already over, but the one between the Sunni and the Shia, which has been marinating for one and a half millennia. We can say, with the facetiousness of despair, that it's just as well to get this out of the way; and let us hope it is merely a Thirty Years War, and not a Hundred Years War. After that, we can look forward to a Renaissance, then a Reformation, followed, in due course, by an Enlightenment. Democracy may then come to the Middle East, with Iraq, in the words of one staffer (a month into the invasion), as the region's "cherished model."

OCTOBER 2006. *The Times*

Demographics

Mark Steyn is an oddity: his thoughts and themes are sane and serious—but he writes like a maniac. A talented maniac; but a maniac. In *America Alone: The End of the World as We Know It,* the central argument gets going, pretty typically, with some reflections on the film *My Big Fat Greek Wedding:*

> Most of us have seen a gazillion heart-warming ethnic comedies . . . in which some uptight WASPy type starts dating a gal from a vast, loving, fecund Mediterranean family, so abundantly endowed with sisters and cousins and uncles that you can barely get in the room. It is, in fact, the inversion of the truth. Greece has a fertility rate hovering just below 1.3 births per couple, which is what demographers call the point of "lowest-low" fertility, from which no human society has ever recovered.

Review of *America Alone: The End of the World as We Know It* by Mark Steyn (Regnery Publishing, Inc., 2006)

And Greece's fertility is the healthiest in Mediterranean
Europe . . .

A "gazillion heart-warming ethnic comedies" with that
storyline? Why, I don't think I've seen even a trillion, or even
a billion, or even a million, or even a thousand, or even a
hundred, or even ten. But never mind for now. The "big Italian family, with Papa pouring out the vino and Mama spoon-
ing out the pasta" down a table that seems to stretch to
infinity, will soon be a thing of the past. By the year 2050,
Steyn spookily informs us, 60 percent of Italians will have no
brothers, no sisters, no uncles, no aunts, and no cousins.

With the sole exception of America, the nations of the
First World are in demographic decline. Not a single Western
European country is procreating at the "replacement rate" of
2.1 births per woman (and the population of Spain, for
instance, will be halving every thirty-five years). This may
seem to be the logical fate of advanced societies on a stressed
planet: there will be crises of distorted age structures and
unaffordable pension liabilities, and so on, but it's the kind of
future envisaged by some of our dreamier greens. We may
note here, incidentally, that Mr. Steyn is a hardy skeptic
about "climate change," and never uses the phrase without
those *noli me tangere* quotation marks. The reader sometimes
feels that *America Alone,* for all its immediacy and glitter, its
stop-press tag lines and flashbulb vulgarisms, went to press in
about 1975. For the author, global warming is the day after
tomorrow (if ever); and we haven't got that long.

A depopulated and simplified Europe might be tenable in a
world without enmity and predation. And that is not our

world. The birth rate is 6.76 in Somalia, 6.69 in Afghanistan, and 6.58 in Yemen. "Notice what these countries have in common?" writes Mr. Steyn, adding, with his usual incontinence: "Starts with an *I* and ends with a *slam*. As in: slam dunk." Albania's birth rate is a third of Afghanistan's, but it's the highest in Europe. "And why would that be? Because it's Europe's only majority Muslim country. At the moment." After Ireland, Denmark, Finland, and Holland, the highest Western European birth rate is that of France, with 1.89. But "the evidence suggests that a third of all births there are already Muslim." Meanwhile:

> Just look at the development within Europe, where the number of Muslims is expanding like mosquitoes. Every Western woman in the EU is producing an average of 1.4 children. Every Muslim in the same countries is producing 3.5 children.

Now those aren't the words of Mr. Steyn—or, say, of Jean-Marie Le Pen. The speaker is Mullah Krekar of Norway. As Colonel Gaddafi puts it: "There are signs that Allah will grant Islam victory in Europe—without swords, without guns, without conquests. The fifty million Muslims of Europe will turn it into a Muslim continent within a few decades."

Any acknowledgment of the fear of being out-bred inevitably reminds us of eugenics and forced sterilization and the like; and many good modern Westerners, reading Mr. Steyn, will feel the warm glow of righteousness that normally precedes an accusation of "racism." As Mr. Steyn patiently insists, however, "it's not about race; it's about culture." If every inhabitant of a liberal democracy believes in liberal democracy, it doesn't matter what creed or color they are; but if some of them believe in sharia and the Caliphate, and so on, then the numbers are clearly crucial. Later in the book, he makes the same point from the other direction. A one-time white-supremacist called David Myatt has changed his name to Abdulaziz ibn Myatt; and Abdulaziz ibn Myatt is a ferocious jihadi. "A lot of his fellow 'white supremacists,'" writes Mr. Steyn, "will find it's not the 'white' but the 'supremacist' bit they really like." Islamism, obviously, will attract the violent. The violent, the pathological, and— needless to say—the anti-Semitic.

So far, the response of the West has been dependably abject. "PC Gone Mad" is of course a cliché—but only because PC goes so mad so often. And Mr. Steyn, as you would expect, has a whale of a time with PCGM (the rebuilding of prison toilets that face away from Mecca, et cetera). But I continue to hope that his admonitions will gain some momentum, despite the efforts of his prose style to impede it. Here is a writer who makes the English language blush at its own vulnerability to pun and play. Two jokes per sentence is the norm, and Mr. Steyn keeps to that ration even when, for example, he is citing the filmed decapitations, in Iraq, of the hostages Ken Bigley and Nick Berg. Why would anyone want a laugh while reading about that? As I closed the book I found myself deciding that Mr. Steyn's sense of decorum must be almost inhumanly thin.

In the U.S., with some Hispanic assistance, the birth rate is 2.1. If we look more closely we see that it's Alabama and

Wyoming we have to thank for that, not California or Massachusetts: the red states are 12 percent more fertile than the blue. According to Mr. Steyn, the "progressive agenda," the culture of rights and entitlements, is "a literal dead end." The unspoken corollary, then, is that societies now need to be more reactionary: patriarchal, churchgoing, majoritarian, and philoprogenitive. *America Alone* is not a long book, and this is just as well: it winds down, about halfway through, into iteration and circularity, without following up on its numerous and grimly riveting implications—among them the completely unsuspected laxity of the urge to reproduce. A practiced sayer of the unsayable, Mr. Steyn nonetheless fails to ask the central question. Will the culture of choice be obliged to give ground to the culture of life?

Itself profoundly retrograde, Islamism may force retrogression on us all. While we're at it, we could take a leaf out of the book of revolutionary Communism. After the startling census of 1936, Stalin immediately abandoned the progressivist social agenda. His new measures included mass kindergartenization, the introduction of maternity medals, the legalization of inheritance, the solemnization of the marriage ceremony, the prolongation and complication of the divorce process, and the recriminalization of abortion. It worked for a while. In the twenty-first century, deprived of totalitarian invigilation, Russia is losing Russians at the rate of about a million a year.

APRIL 2007. *The Times*

On the Move with Tony Blair

No. 1, London

It isn't bad, driving through town with Tony. The car's steel cladding, as the P.M. points out, is almost comically thick — so thick, indeed, that the interior has the feel of something like a Ford Fiesta rather than a Jaguar; and it takes nearly all your strength to tug shut the slablike door behind you. But then we're away. The crouched policemen, in their dayglo yellow strip, buzz past like purposeful hornets to liberate the road ahead. We barely brake once between Downing Street and the Westway. The power is ebbing from him now; but for a little while longer we can luxuriate in the present tense. And, yes, it's a bit of all right, driving through town with Tony.

The best moment comes as we approach Hyde Park Corner. Instead of toiling around it, like all the other fools and losers, we sail *across* it, diagonally, under the arch and the jagged, power-mad neoclassical statue (Apollo on his chariot with the four horses), and then curve right past that far from unfashionable address—No. 1, London. We are talking about Islamism in Britain, and Tony, when on the move, has this much in common with British Islamists: he habitually jumps red lights. Islamists do it to show contempt for the law of the land (and contempt for reason). Tony does it to thwart Islamists.

Now I notice that the P.M. wears no seat belt. When I tenderly point this out to him, he gives an unemphatic shrug. He is, he says, "embarrassed by the bikes." I am wondering if that's why Tony looks so young—ten years in a world without traffic. But it wasn't always like this. The police escort, like so much else, is a consequence of September 11.

In Conversation

Blair was in Brighton on that day, preparing to give a humdrum speech to the Trades Union Congress. He delivered his speech, a different speech (more urgent, and much shorter), then took the train back to London and started trying to raise George Bush.

"Did you sense at the time that September 11 would . . . define your premiership?"

"Yes, I think I did. And I was already sure that Islamic fundamentalism would be *huge*. Infinite demands, to be achieved by any means whatever. That's quite a combination."

As we neared the RAF airbase I said cautiously, "Was it realized, in 2003, that a democratic Mesopotamia would give rise to something unprecedented? I mean a Shia Arab state."

Blair waited. Interviewing the P.M., I was often disconcerted to find that I was doing most of the talking. I said,

"The insurgency is partly a spoiling operation. The Sunni elite think the Shia are scum. They say, 'We rule. They wail.' The equivalent here—and there's no inoffensive way of putting this—would be having the Travelers' Party in power. You know: the nut-rissole artists." And you wouldn't like that, would you? "The Sunni are more legalistic. The Shia are dreamier and more poetic and emotional. Are you talking to Iran?"

"There are feelers about opening a back channel. But in my experience back channels to Iran always turn out to be bullshit."

We got on the plane and flew to Germany. When it comes to the consumption of alcohol, George Bush, of course, makes Tony Blair look like Boris Yeltsin. But in truth Blair hardly touches the stuff. On the roof of the vast Chancellery (six times the size of the White House), in Berlin, I did see him nurse a glass of beer during his tête-à-tête with Angela Merkel—a measure, perhaps, of how charmed and stimulated he is by her. And Angela is known to like a drop.

"Germany is obsessed by transparency," I had said to him. "Some think it's because what it fears most is itself."

"That view's old-fashioned," said Blair.

Edinburgh

We were at the Corn Exchange, where Tony would soon denounce the Scots Nats (its separatist policy he characterized as "disastrous in its consequences and reactionary in its soul"). During the pre-speech lull he strolled over and said,

"*I* had a shock this morning."

Yes, I thought: I should just about say you *did* have a shock this morning. I almost said, "I saw it, mate." Because there it stood on the front page of *The Independent*: the shadowy photograph (making him look haunted, hunted—isolated, above all) and the banner headline, "BLAIRAQ." "An exclusive poll reveals that 69 percent of Britons believe that, when he leaves office, his enduring legacy will be . . ." But it was, of course, laughably inexperienced of me to think that this was the shock Tony hoped to discuss. He's not about to *raise* the subject of Iraq. Everyone else on earth can be depended on to do that. It is impossible to exaggerate it: the white-lipped and bloody-minded persistence of the subject of Iraq.

"I went on GMTV," he continued, moving his head about stiffly in mock indignation, "and Kate Moss's models were on it too. Five or six of them. And all of them amazingly beautiful."

"Wearing?"

"Not much. They were all about six foot three. In incredibly short skirts. And someone said, 'Did you notice how short their skirts were?' And I said, 'No! No!'"

"Bit early in the day," grumbled my colleague (and exact contemporary: closer to sixty than fifty).

"Oh," said the P.M., "it wasn't too early in the day."

One should be careful not to misrepresent our famously uxorious Prime Minister. His manner wasn't lewd or even laddish; it was merely youthful. Tall, but not imposingly tall, slightly pigeon-toed in gait, with surprisingly full, clean, kind blue eyes, Blair makes you think that the words "boy-ish" and "buoyant" must have a common root. As you get older, it's not just the policemen who get younger: it's also the prime ministers. And I'm being ruled, I suddenly think, by a prefect.

"No," he concluded, shaking his head. "It never is too early in the day."

And it never *was* too early in the day. Too early for me—but not for him. That morning, after a long speech (and Q and A) at the King's Fund on the gripping theme of the NHS, and then the appearance on GMTV, Tony showed up for a raucous bash at Labour HQ—and it was barely 8:30. Disco music on the turquoise boombox! The coffees! The teas! That exclusive *Independent* poll also revealed, much more quietly, that 61 percent of Britons believe Blair to have been "a good prime minister," including 89 percent of Labour supporters. This ardor was palpable. The warm-up act came courtesy of Old Labour, in the person of that battered sensualist John Prescott ("A decade of delivery!"); then the crowd, audibly gurgling with adoration, feasted its senses on the P.M.

The smart open-plan office they were standing in represents a further concretization of what Blair has done for the party. Until 1995, Labour was stationed in Walworth Road, SE17, a facility described at the time as "crap" by Blair and as "fuck-awful" by Alastair Campbell. From the old HQ—remote, poky, dank with lumpen defeat—the foot soldiers got their upgrade: to Millbank Tower, just across the river from Parliament. Then came the mighty computer, "Excalibur," primed for lightspeed rebuttal of all Tory boasts and smears. The symbolism was unambiguous: here was electoral modernity, and the party machine.

Blair "chose" Labour, but reinvented himself as its
antithesis. A mutant: something like an upper-middle-class
German-American Christian Democrat. Compared to him,
Gordon Brown is all fish-and-chips and Woodbines. But the
party loves the P.M., not least because he *is* the P.M., and
goes on being the P.M.: he is their redeemer, their awakener,
their landslider.

"I know what TV stands for," I said to an aide. "But what
does GM stand for? I've been away."

"Good Morning."

"I see. Thanks," I said. It was ten to nine.

At the Point Conference Centre in Edinburgh, during
another lull, Tony strolled over once again and said, "What
have you been up to today?"

"I've been feeling protective of my Prime Minister, since
you ask." For some reason our acquaintanceship, at least on
my part, is becoming mildly but deplorably flirtatious.
"You've had reverses in the midterms before. And in the
European Parliament. But this will probably be your first . . .
rejection."

"This won't be my first rejection. 2004. 2002."

"Cheriegate? That was bullshit, right?"

"Oh, *complete* bullshit. But what about you?" he typically
asks (no reader himself, he is, nonetheless, habitually or even
instinctively empathetic). "If your books get attacked, you
don't let it throw you."

The P.M. had earlier confessed that it wasn't just the
miniskirts that gave him a turn on GMTV. There was also

the contrast between his face on the monitor and all that bright and breezy footage from 1997: "The ageing process on screen," he said. It wasn't a before-and-after such as Abe Lincoln's—the handsome frontiersman completely desiccated by the Civil War. Whatever way you look at it, though, ten years is a long time, and not just in politics.

"There's also an ageing process within," I said. "You don't get tougher. You get tenderer. And certain phrases come into your head. Like 'life's work.'" Yes, or like "legacy." "But you've got steel. Like your car."

"Mm. Armor-plated."

It was hardly necessary to point to the differences of scale. I suppose that Salman Rushdie and Orhan Pamuk, and others, have been reluctantly obliged to gain an inkling of how politicians sometimes feel. But more generally a book review is not a plebiscite, a million-man march, a flag-draped casket, a country—perhaps a region—consigned to the flames and the sword.

The Den

Number 10 Downing Street, broad, tall, and deep, has the appearance of a country hotel, with the furnishings of a Harley Street waiting room; and there is a mid-stairs feel to it. You go past the discreetly burping doorman, and for every striding or trotting secretary ("Is the P.M. still in there?"), for every spin doctor and dreamily cruising technocrat, there's a bloke trundling past with a rubbish barrel or a porter's trolley.

You feel at once that the atmosphere is also palpably civil and tolerant and quasi-egalitarian. "Tony," a staffer told me, "is a great non-belittler." Downing Street, after all, is presided over by a man who answers to a diminutive (and will go down in history with that forename). This may have been notionally true under Ted Heath and Jim Callaghan, but not under, say, Dai Lloyd George, Andy Bonar Law, Stan Baldwin, Nev Chamberlain, Winnie Churchill, Harry Wilson, or, for that matter, Tony Eden.

"There it is," said Tony. "You can sit on it. The famous *sofa*."

"Ah yes. The famous *sofa*. Do you mind if I don't use a tape recorder?"

The Tony administration, some say, deploys a "sofa" style of governance: the normal channels of influence are largely bypassed, and the P.M. depends on his inner circle of brainstormers and media-wise myrmidons. In May–June 1997 it was decided that the regulation of interest rates should be depoliticized and become the responsibility of the Bank of England; when Tony was forewarned that such a momentous change should be discussed with Cabinet, he said, "Oh they won't mind. We'll ring round."

Today I was allowed into the Den to witness "Denocracy" (another name for it) in action. The subject was climate change and exploratory talks on the creation of a "carbon market." Tony listened to six or seven voices ("Those two are still slagging each other off . . . Chancellor Merkel wants a deal . . . The meeting with the Indians was positive . . . The Japanese was extremely touchy . . . The American was extremely difficult"), before weighing in with his summary and conclusion: "We need to make it clear what it means for

American business—that they won't leach contracts to the Chinese. I will work it through with him. With Bush."

Then it was upstairs to the White Room for a podcast with Bob Geldof on Africa—Africa, a quarter-century compulsion of Geldof's and a solid ten-year enthusiasm of Blair's. Then it was downstairs to the long table and a multinational convocation of bishops. Power has been described as a drug, an aphrodisiac, a "filthy venom" (in the words of Maxim Gorky); it is also, for much of the time, carcinogenically boring. Like all politicians, Tony has seven or eight kinds of smile. Smiles two and three would do for the bishops (and for the convocation of bishops, I thought, well, he has his religion to help him through it). More generally, when he is making the rounds of a crowded room, his smile, toward the end, is a rictus, and his eyes are as hard as jewels.

All the boredom is what the world doesn't see—the hidden toil of dosing and humoring, of giving face and jollying along. It is this that keeps politicians halfway honest, and impedes the process that Bob Geldof alluded to, up in the White Room: "It's a bit naff, isn't it? What happened? The politicization of celebrity or the celebritization of politics?" And the question arose: What will Tony be, when he quits? An ex-politician?

"No," he said. "I'll be a former celebrity."

Belfast

Riding in the convoy—from George Best Belfast City Airport to Stormont Castle—was, as usual, no fun at all. Sometimes you are doing seventy miles an hour, and the breaking distance between you and perdition falls well below the eighty-odd yards recommended by my Highway Code: it is ten or twelve feet. The convoy drivers are trained to dispense with peripheral vision, and fixate on the hideously proximate backside of the jeep in front. It is an obsession that the passenger soon learns to share.

And there was the castle, a thrillingly emotive sight on this day—the great dripping edifice of intransigence. But now what? As the motorcade came up the mile-long Stormont Road, flailing figures twirled out at us, with impressive menace and address, and there was a bit of warm work for the sweating policemen: a bit of buffeting, bear-hugging, and rugby-tackling. Were these flailers and twirlers the representatives of all the diehards and bitter-enders who want a return to the Troubles? No. They were here for Iraq.

Within, Blair knocked off some interviews before the historic addresses in the Great Hall. And I spent the time trying to parse the anarchy of his accent, a dog's breakfast of Durham, public-school Edinburgh, Australia (years one to four), and estuary Essex. "Wanted" is *wantud,* and "destructive" is *destructuv.* The terminal *t* is regularly swallowed ("it's nok clear") and there is a candid glottal stop in his *wha'ever* (in contrast to his prissy use of the archaic *whilst*). Blair was reminiscing about his childhood holidays in Donegal and his first "half" of *Guinnuss* when, ineluctably, the interviewer said, "One last question, Prime Minister. This is a huge achievement, but it seems your main legacy will be . . ." And Blair's blue eyes minutely flinch, and seem to cancel themselves.

I watched the swearing-in at the Assembly by TV link, and it was something to see. The faces of the hoary politicos, rendered scalene by ancient stubbornnesses—but now uncertainly smiling. The old zealot Paisley, still cake-in-the-rain handsome in his eighty-first year. The affectless Martin McGuinness of Sinn Fein, a ringer for Conrad's "Professor," the meager megalomaniac in *The Secret Agent* whose "thoughts caressed the images of ruin and destruction." But there we had it, the convergence of the twain, in an atmosphere of long-compressed agitation and near-hilarity, the hilarity of the unreal.

Meanwhile, outside, a reminder of local concerns: NO SHRINE AT THE MAZE and JUSTICE FOR PROTESTANTS and several capitalized gripes about the water rates. But the big banner, and all the energy, proclaimed: BLAIR LEGACY 600,000 DEAD IN IRAQ. And at the next stop, a courtesy call at the venerable daily *The News Letter,* there was a raggedly thrashing figure on the street with a policeman sitting on it and a police dog barking at it, and BLIAR. WANTED. WAR CRIMINAL.

We are witnesses to the triumphal speeches and we hear the applause, but we don't usually see the moment of fierce political relish, the deep and durable gloat of *vindication:* I was right all along! At another castle, Hillsborough (the Queen's Belfast bolt-hole and Bush's occasional crashpad), there was one such, when Blair had a quiet half-hour with the tottering Teddy Kennedy and the redoubtable Peter Hain. History—the remorseless unforeseen—had for once in its life colluded with their desire, and it was all very understated, this forgivable preen, all very hushed and husky and hard-won.

Kennedy said that he had been involved in the process since Bloody Sunday in 1972 (Blair's gap year: he was a velvet-looned Bee Gee with a guitar called Clarence). Thirteen died on Bloody Sunday; and the toll for the whole period stands at about 3,500—or the equivalent of one bad month in Iraq. Later, in Basra, Blair would tell the troops that the struggle they were engaged in was "infinitely more important than Northern Ireland," for the simple reason that it would shape "the future of the world."

On the plane, in a brief audience with the P.M., I said that the events of the day were of course exhilarating, but they taught an ominous lesson. How long does it take to evolve from terror to politics? Could he imagine, in the Iraqi parliament of the future, the ghosts of Moqtada al-Sadr and Abu Musab al-Zarqawi smiling at each other with Irish eyes?

"It must happen," he said. "Something like that must eventually happen."

In Conversation—2

"The massive stroke suffered by your father. He was forty. You were eleven. And in the morning your mother came into the room. And as you said later, 'She hadn't even spoken and I was in tears . . .' "

"That's right. I could tell by her face that something absolutely *awful* had happened."

"Your mother reminds me of my mother. A saint but not a martyr."

"That's an accurate description of her."

"And she died very early, didn't she? At fifty-two. There

have been many early deaths, early incapacitations, in your life story. Do you think that caused you to be . . . more driven?"

Blair did that thing you read about in novels: he twisted in his seat. He is made uneasy by the Freudian innuendo; he is made uneasy by the personal. It would be a waste of time to ask him about Cherie. Or about Gordon Brown (their relationship, I decided, had turned into something like a ten-year divorce between fraternal twins who happened to be married to each other). And I found, after a while, that I had stopped making notes: I wasn't getting anything I hadn't heard elsewhere. But I made one final try.

"It was your mother, Hazel, who was the religious one. And then you got *more* religious at Oxford."

"Religion was in the air then. Like politics—something you talked about late at night."

"And yours is a practical kind of religion, isn't it? Communitarianism . . ."

"Communitarianism. The individual and society. Values."

"Do you believe in a supernatural being?"

He twisted in his seat.

"Do you believe in an afterlife?"

He twisted in his seat.

"And all your trusted people are secularists," I said. "You're surrounded by secularists." Who, I thought, must spend much of the time rolling their eyes.

"Funnily enough," he said, "the one who had most sympathy for it was Alastair Campbell."

Alastair Campbell, who notoriously and brutishly told the press, "We don't *do* religion."

Blair went on, "Alastair was sympathetic, but he said, 'Look. This isn't America. Religion and politics don't mix.'"

"And when religion and politics mix?"

"You start saying things like 'God made me do it.'"

Washington

"Sit Room" is not an American contraction along the lines of *fry pan, sleep pill,* or *shave cream.* Far from being the sitting room, the Sit Room is the Situation Room, where, this morning, Bush and Blair, and Condi and Cheney, are having a video teleconference with their commanders and ambassadors in Iraq. Any moment now there will be an elaborately staged side-by-side, shoulder-to-shoulder double-premier advance to the Oval Office for talks, with other participants, about Africa, Iran, and "energy security." The atmosphere in these corridors, the aides, the secret-service men, the odd wandering pol with hair as rigid as caramel or marzipan, doesn't remind you of anything else. A futuristic academy, perhaps, of pure power.

The style is not prime-ministerial but presidential: at every moment the office itself is honored and exalted. You get a sense of it on Pennsylvania Avenue, where, with your press cards (plural), your staff pin, and your photo ID, you confront the scowling, head-shaking jacks-in-office at the gate — incarnations of disgusted skepticism. The whole place fizzes with zero tolerance, with the prideful tension and frigidity of high protocol. Its peculiarly American flavor is evident in the sustained choreography, and the dread of the spontaneous. This *does* remind you of something: a film set. After prodigious delays and innumerable false alarms, and bungled rehearsals (with stand-ins), Harrison Ford and Hugh Grant give us their fifteen seconds, then it's back to the delays and the false alarms and the bungled rehearsals.

Pretty well everyone, from the semi-literate windbags of the blogosphere ("So! The poddle of Downing Street once agian feel's the tug of his masters leish!") to King Abdullah of Saudi Arabia (who has started defying the Americans because he "doesn't want to be known as the Arab Tony Blair"), pretty well everyone agrees that the P.M. has vitiated his premiership by cleaving too close to George Bush—an association described as "tragic" by Neil Kinnock and "abominable" by Jimmy Carter. And Blair himself, I thought, was arrestingly forthright when he said, in a recent interview on NBC, that "at one level . . . it is the job of the British Prime Minister to get on with the American President." This is a tradition that goes back, with certain fluctuations, to Churchill and the termination of Britain's imperial sway. One should not pretend that it is a frictionless business, saying no to America. It is one thing to be "a leading member of the EU." It is quite another to be what Clinton called "the world's one indispensable nation."

I am given a clandestine glimpse of this disparity in the Roosevelt Room, while chewing on a bonbon graciously offered to me by a passing Karl Rove ("We need a little glucose here"), and waiting for Harrison and Hugh to start their next scene. A few prime-ministerial staffers are comparing notes with a presidential equivalent on the question of foreign travel. When Blair goes somewhere, he relies on a staff

of thirty (and five bodyguards). When Bush goes somewhere, he relies on a staff of 800 (and 100 bodyguards); and if
he visits two countries on the same trip, the figure is 1,600;
three countries, and the figure is 2,400. Having reached his
destination, Blair will throw in his lot with whatever transport is made available. Using military aircraft, Bush takes
along his own limousine, his own backup limousine, his own
refueling trucks, and his own helicopters. "Mm," murmurs a
chastened Brit. "You make our lives seem very simple." This,
shall we say, is the diplomatic way of putting it.

Lurking in a Roosevelt Room doorway, I am privileged to
receive a two-second once-over from the President as he and
Blair make their stately way from the Sit Room; I admit, for
what it's worth, that I inclined my head at him. I am also
allowed a couple of minutes in the Oval Office as the princi-
pals take their seats. And there is an *incident*.

"Did you hear that?" a Blair liaison officer later asks me.

"Yes, I did."

"Do you intend to put it in your piece?"

"Yeah, I thought I might."

"Don't."

"Why not?"

"Don't."

And I obeyed—though of course I have no compunction
about slinging it in here. Bush was saying, of something or
other, "I've never seen so much bullshit in my life." Then,
much more interestingly, he jerked to his feet, yelling at the
cameraman, "Give me the tape! Give me the tape!" That is to
say, the President was going to confiscate the evidence—the
evidence of his profanity. Blair's people didn't want to add to

Bush's problems. No headlines saying, "Prez in 'Bullshit' Storm." No month-long frenzy of bullshit about the "bullshit." Every little helps—what with the 30 percent approval rating, the dead-duck second term, the double-or-quits "surge" in Iraq.

Bush and Blair exchanged their political farewells at a press conference in the Rose Garden. The President, by now, fancies himself a great wit (among other things), having spent six years surrounded by people who double up at his feeblest crack. But it has to be said that Bush was at his very best that day, generous and affectionate, and quick to acknowledge the political pain he had inflicted on his (necessarily) junior partner. Then, too, there were the coded salutes to Blairean "influence" in Bush's mention of global warming ("a serious issue") and his tolerant reference to the two-state solution in the Middle East.

The P.M., for his part, gave a passionate restatement of his crystallized rationale: after September 11, the West had no choice but to unite against a planetary enemy; and he did what he did because he believed it was right. While the two men spoke you could hear the distant bawling of the protestors on Pennsylvania Avenue. It was as if an incensed but microscopic goblin was off in the bushes somewhere, down by the ornamental lake, his voice strained to the maximum yet barely louder than the endless miaows of the cameras.

After a session at the British Embassy celebrating Northern Ireland, we were given the full totalitarian motorcade from Massachusetts Avenue to Andrews Air Force Base. At every crossroads, junction, and side-turning there was a square-on squad car keeping the lid on a half-mile Tony tailback. And on we sped—our limousines, our Rolls-Royce, our SWAT truck—across the overpass above a Beltway shorn of all traffic, and onto the tarmac where our plane would take us, via Heathrow, to Kuwait City.

Here's something that I bet Tony's people didn't dare tell George's people. The plane we're flying in (an executive jet with three classes and a little bedroom for the P.M.) was chartered, on the open market, from a company based in the Middle East.

In Conversation—3

After the ten-hour flight from Washington, we had time for a coffee and a biscuit on that strange surface, solid ground (in a joint called the Royal Suite at Heathrow), before wisely returning to the plane for the ten-hour flight to the Gulf. On the way I was to have my heart-to-heart with Tony on Iraq.

Giving an informal speech in Northern Ireland, the P.M. told of the time at Hillsborough Castle when, after a long night of negotiations, he went upstairs to find Ken McGinnis (a formidably butch politico) asleep in his bed. "I am devoted to the cause," he said—but not *that* devoted . . . We had just finished lunch, somewhere over the Balkans, when I was asked to step forward; and I wistfully wondered if Tony and I would have our chat in all the privacy and comfort of his little love nest near the cockpit. But no. I rose from my seat in business (coach, normally empty, was crammed with extra press, most of it televisual), and went forward to Blair's throne in first.

"What would have been the price of saying no to America?"

"Saying no to America would have been huge."

"Didn't Jack Straw say we would 'reap a whirlwind'?"

"It is very, very difficult to say no to America. It would have meant staying out of the aftermath. It would have meant not being involved."

"I suppose we're all involved. There are no Switzerlands in this fight."

"I don't know about *Switzerland,*" he said, not wishing, presumably, to offend the Swiss. "But yes. There are no neutralist positions."

Blair would agree, perhaps, that he played his hand too early. He committed himself to Washington before securing a) a promise to push for a broader coalition, and b) linkage with what statesmen call MEPP (the Middle East Peace Process). But wasn't the tempo of the whole effort fatally brisk? I said,

"Everything that went wrong went wrong because of tempo, didn't it? Even Abu Ghraib. No trained interrogators and no interpreters. Just Mr. and Mrs. Lynndie England."

"Yes, well, the pace of it . . ."

It was the tempo, the pace, the rush—the power rush. We talked on. Hereafter he made only one statement that I hadn't heard before. He said,

"Al-Qaeda actions are treated as morally neutral. They're treated like natural disasters."

Or like acts of God. Where were we—over Turkey? Over

Syria? Below, the clouds presided over their shadows on the sand.

"You don't lose your emotional response," he said, "but you can't lose your nerve. You get to the point where you're unable to do the job unless you're prepared to make the decisions of life and death."

Iraq

My support for the war, non-existent until it actually began, received no noticeable fillip as I donned my ten-kilo combat vest (as if in preparation for a viciously searching X-ray) and my flak helmet, and trudged up into the rump of the Hercules C-130—for the flight from Kuwait City to Baghdad. It didn't feel like a plane. It felt like a hangar.

I had earlier been roused by a 4:30 wake-up call, and had then extracted a) two bottles of water from a minibar childishly infested with 7UPs and Oranginas, and b) a full toilet roll from the adjacent bathroom (what I really wanted was a Depend Undergarment). My breakfast, too, was untypically light on the All-Bran and the cups of fuming black coffee. We gathered in the forecourt and advanced to the airport, by humble motor coach, through the almost artistic cheerlessness of the Kuwaiti capital—a conurbation seemingly put together, from top to bottom, without a woman's touch, its only colors commercial, its only curves devotional, under a sinister mist of damp dust.

The interior of the Hercules was without surfaces; it was all innards—sacking, wiring, tubing, webbing. DANGER,

WARNING, EMERGENCY GROUND, and DITCH. A soldier hollered out our survival instructions, not a word of which I caught, and of course there were no tranquil updates from the captain, and no accessible portholes, so the only progress reports were acoustical: fantastic snortings and screechings, as in some low-mimetic science-fictional piece about a ravaged freighter toiling through the intergalactic voids. Another novelty was the direction of the G-forces, which came at you sideways-on, bending your torso to the right as the plane lifted off, then to the left as it walloped back to earth.

Tony rode in the cockpit, and spiffily disembarked, at Baghdad International, in suit and tie. At no point, so far as I saw, did he encumber himself with the neck-ricking headgear or the snarling Velcro of the flak jacket. And I remembered that first journey when, in rather more agreeable surroundings, he disdained the use of the seat belt in his armor-plated Jag. What is this prime-ministerial trait? The rest of us, by this stage, were carapaced in sweat and grit. But not Tony. Rumor predicts that on his retirement Blair will seek solace, along with his wife, in the bosom of Rome. But surely he is Calvinism incarnate—the central doctrine being that your salvation is secured *by your confidence in it*. In Iraq, Tony crossed the runway like a true exceptionalist: one of the chosen, the redeemed, the elect.

Needless to say, there would be no eye-catching motorcade for "the Highway of Death" to Baghdad. Tony climbed into his Black Hawk; I climbed into my Cobra, and watched, with fatalistic detachment, as the tawny teenager fed the cartridge belt into the tripod-mounted machine gun. We steered low, just above the telegraph wires. At this height (I was told), no missile would have time to arm itself before impact. The Cobra would take the hit, but it wouldn't actually explode. Perfect, perfect: I couldn't feel more secure. We also fired off flares as we flew, so that the enemy projectile, with implausible credulity, would seek their heat rather than ours—the baby firework rather than its farting, yammering sire. If you closed your eyes you seemed to hear music, military but atonal, like tinnitus.

Mortar fire had just savaged a Toyota Land Cruiser in the parking lot of the British Embassy, our first stop in the Green Zone. While Tony took his rictus and his frozen eyes from handshake to handshake, I got talking to Jackie, a member of the managerial staff. "Every day now we have an *incoming*," she said. "For six weeks we've been getting it. If you're inside you're all right. It's the hot metal—the shrapnel. If you're outside there are these duck-and-cover units. They're like boxes, and you're supposed to scramble into them when you hear the five-second warning. You don't bother if you've got a clean white skirt on."

We bustled ahead, in stop-start convoy, to a press conference at the unpalatial "palace," or the Prime Minister's residence: heavy sofas, gilt-trimmed chandeliers, artificial roses, artificial light. Al-Maliki shuffled along the damp red carpet to greet and kiss the grandly waddling figure of President Talabani, and they disappeared behind the inevitable stockade of TV cameras. There were hostile questions, and you could hear Blair's weak protesting treble and Talabani's didactic baritone: progress, improvement, the Iraqi security forces, the dialogue with the tribes, constructive talks, the way forward, the channel to Iran . . . We shunted on to Maud House, HQ of the British Support Unit, just in time for another alert. General David Petraeus—Wolfowitzian in appearance, with a nervous, wincing laugh—barely blinked as the sirens took up their weary and long-suffering squawk.

"It's *Apocalypse Now* meets Disneyland": this was the twinkly verdict of a British staff colonel. And there came an interlude, on the helipad (like a drained swimming pool of gray concrete, the size of a city block), where you could find some shade and try to bring order to the skein of impressions and the vague, persistent tickle of the unreal. The Green Zone resembles the embassy district of a minor South American capital after a period of immiseration and collapse, where the powers that be, or the powers that remain, are exhaustedly girding themselves for the chaos and butchery of revolution. I found myself staring at a discarded ornamental armchair (its symbolism all too cooperative), which grimly presided over a heap of undifferentiated rubbish. Then it was wheels up, nose down, and we clattered over Baghdad, the apartment blocks like low-rise car parks, with trash everywhere, and greenmantled standing pools.

Something happened to Blair in Basra—at the airport base, which is pretty well all that's left of the operation in the south, the city having been abandoned to the general atomization: Shia factions, tribal militias, armed gangs. There had been several hundred handshakes in the coffee bar (the old VIP room in which many Iraqis once braced themselves for the hajj), and several hundred ten-second conversations; there had been a reasonably good speech, reasonably well received. Blair then repaired to a side room, for a closed session—with the padre, several officers, and about twenty-five young soldiers. And something happened.

There was a haunting paragraph from the padre about "the hard and dark side" of recent events at the camp (many losses, many unspeakable injuries), about transformative experiences, about the way "these young people have had to grow up very quickly." And when it came to Blair—all the oxygen went out of him. It wasn't just that he seemed acutely underbriefed (on munitions, projects, tactics). He was quite unable to find weight of voice, to find decorum, the appropriate words for the appropriate mood. "So we kill more of them than they kill us . . . You're getting back out there and after them. It's brilliant, actually . . ." The P.M., it has to be said, appeared to be the least articulate man in the room. The least articulate—and also the *youngest*.

I stayed on after Blair took his leave. Two minutes later there was a room-jarring *whump*. "Sit on the floor, everyone," drawled the officer. As we hunkered down, the boyish corporal I was talking to, without a second's pause (so routine was the interruption), went on telling me about the firepower of the Tomahawk anti-tank guided missile. I said goodbye, after the all-clear, to those earnestly frowning faces, those men of impressive, indeed daunting steadfastness and altruism; and our party filed out, leaving them there in a desert both spiritual and actual, under the thick, dirty-white medium of sand and dust, like soiled medical gauze coming down to cover the breath. We climbed back into the Hercules and strapped ourselves in for the thirty-minute ride to Kuwait City.

Person to Person

"This is Downing Street and there's nobody home," runs the joke. "Please leave a message after the high moral tone." The high moral tone, such an infuriant to his detractors, is not something that Blair has co-opted, to round out the panoply of his merits. Like his religion it is entirely innate: if that wasn't there, nothing else would be there. He has been called a Manichee, seeing only light and darkness; and he has been called an antinomian, a self-angelizer who holds that what he does is right by virtue of the fact that he does it. This is the mechanism Blair is reduced to, I think, in his rationale for Iraq. The forces of darkness are arrayed against the forces of light; and we cannot afford to lose. Both propositions, in my opinion, are perfectly true. We cannot afford to lose, but lose we will, in this theater of the Coalition's misdirected choosing.

I had that hour on Iraq, person to person; and there were other duologues. Except at odd moments, though, in corridors and anterooms, you never are person to person with Tony Blair. There is always the photographer, the documentarist, the aide with the tape recorder and the stopwatch. There is also the professionalized superego of the P.M., schooled in caution, incessantly aware that his airiest word can double back on him and loom like a Saturn. It is not the case, as the dulled phrase has it, that what you see is what you get: he is more physically impressive, more sensitive, and much more playful than the man on your TV screen. But it remains true, with Blair, that what you hear is what you hear.

"Have you seen *The Queen*?" I asked him. We were flying

to Germany, on one of the old, slow Hawker Siddeleys, borrowed from the royal fleet (she's the head of state, remember,
and just completing her eleventh term). The crested anti-
macassars, the scones served with cream and jam. You feel
you're on an old-style railway train—say, the Brighton
Belle, which, had it lived on, might have brought Blair back
to London on September 11.

"Uh—no."

"Well, it's a case of everyone getting everything wrong.
Helen Mirren is as usual a pleasure to watch. But she's a *hope-
less* Elizabeth. All that wryness and irony. I've met the
Queen, for about ten seconds, and she's completely un-
reflecting. She's a heifer. Don't you think?"

"I won't be going along with *that,*" he said, not unamused,
but twisting in his seat more violently than ever.

"But you, *you.* The actor gets you to the life. The sheen of
youth. The sheen of power." I was reminded, later, that the
actor is even called Michael Sheen. "What's it like, power?
Lenin said it made the head spin. Is it heady?"

"Yes, but you're stabilized by the responsibility. I like to
think I can do without it. You have to be able to risk it, and
leave some room for instinctive judgement. You have to face
the possibility of losing it. In order to use it."

"Those autographs for my daughters," I said, in the Den at
Downing Street, much later on but before the day trip to
Iraq. "They'll kill me if I forget. Just scribble them on my pad
here."

"Oh no. We'll need prime-ministerial paper for this."

"The little one wants your phone number too. She's seven.
Expect her call."

"I think the number's on the letterhead. No: just the address." He looked up with obliging expectancy. "So it's . . . Fernanda?"

"Yes. And the little one. With an *i,* not an *e*." And, no, there never is any respite. "Clio," I said. "The muse of history."

". . . Clio. There we are."

"So how does it feel, now that it's ebbing from you? Power."

"All right so far. When the day comes I'll probably be clinging to the door knocker. 'I'm homeless!' But so far I think I can just . . . let it go."

JUNE 2007. *The Guardian*

An Islamist's Journey

This is hearsay, but I have heard it said that the Islamist recruitment gambit, or chat-up line, seldom varies. You are a young British Muslim, in London or Leeds, and you are toweling yourself down after a ping-pong tournament or a paintball fest at your community center, and another young British Muslim wanders up to you and says, in the accent of Leeds or London, "Heard about the Caliphate, mate?"

"You what?"

"The Caliphate. The *Khalifah*."

The Caliphate, as every Islamist is bitterly aware, was dissolved by Kemal Atatürk on March 3, 1924. It is the Islamists' intention to restore the sultan as the head of a nation state, a nation state of science-fictional power, which will (if I've got this right) wage jihad on all the world.

Ed Husain's *The Islamist* is a tale of gradual radicalization, of cheerful and wholehearted fanaticism, of crisis and disillu-

Review of *The Islamist: Why I Joined Radical Islam in Britain, What I Saw Inside and Why I Left* by Ed Husain (Penguin Books, 2007)

sion, and of gradual and painful decontamination. British by
birth and Indo-Pakistani by descent, Husain was an obedient
child who, during adolescence, came under the sway of a *pir,*
or mystic master. Fultholy Saheb taught little Ed *tajwid,* or
the art of Koranic recital; other routines included *dhikr*
(chanting the Arabic names of God in the dark) and *mawlid*
(rehearsing the miracles that attended the Prophet's birth). Ed
loved the attention, and the sense of unity. "In many ways,"
he writes, "I suppose I was a sort of Muslim choirboy."

With his piety and thick spectacles, the growing Husain
was a bullied loner at Stepney Green Secondary. While his
contemporaries affiliated themselves with the Brick Lane
Mafia or the Bow Massive, Husain signed up with the Young
Muslim Organization, whose members seemed as "bad and
cool as the other street gangs, just without the drugs, drink-
ing, and womanizing." The YMO owed allegiance to the
Jamaat-e-Islami, founded in 1941 by a Pakistani journalist
called Abul Ala Mawdudi, who championed a politicized
Islam as "a complete code of life." Husain's parents, and his
pir, would have been less horrified if he had joined the Can-
non Street Posse.

An ideology is in the business of aggrandizing those who
subscribe to it, and Husain was soon assured that he was
vastly superior to pretty well everyone, all women ("women
are the plague"), all Jews (of course), all *kafirs* (or *koofs*), and
all "partial Muslims," like his mother and father (soon to be
jettisoned). Endearingly, though, the tenor of Husain's teenage years goes on seeming reasonably teenage. Whereas other
boys smuggled pornography into their rooms, "my contra-
band consisted of books written by Islamist ideologues."

Turning to a more radical mosque, he can pray bareheaded without messing up his hairstyle. Islamist chicks, in their *jilbabs* and *niqabs,* are far more alluring than all those *kafir* nudists. Spurning both promiscuity and arranged marriages, Islamists tend to elope; and divorce rates among them, Husain reveals, are un-Islamically high. The more common pattern—Husain's pattern—is to keep your sexual tension stoppered, and work it off with religious rage.

In organizational terms, Islamism is Leninist. The radicals, with their advanced consciousness, form a vanguard, and seek power in the name, not of the supranational proletariat, but of the *umma,* the supranational community of believers. Reliant on cadres (*halaqahs*), fiercely destructive in debate, and desperately alert to "deviation," the Mawdudis, Wahhabis, and Nabhanis are as fissiparous as the Bolsheviks, the Mensheviks, and the Socialist-Revolutionists of 1917. "The YMO are a bunch of losers," Husain is eventually told. The time has come for him to hear about the Caliphate. We now rise up into a new echelon. This is a creedal movement vigorously suppressed in all Muslim countries, but not here—the Hizb ut-Tahrir.

I think we may be putting it mildly when we say that the Hizb vision remains slightly counter-intuitive. Well, here is Husain at his most enthusiastic about what he grandly calls "the *khalifah* system":

We were singleminded in our pursuit of establishing a clear Islamic state, for in the obtaining of political power lay all the answers to the problems of the Muslim nation. Our arguments were powerful and, at first, undefeatable. "If we had the Islamic state, then the Caliph would send the Islamic army to slaughter the Serbs," was our answer to the Balkan conflict . . . More precisely, our foreign policy was to conquer and convert.

The Islamic state—soon to appear, probably by coup, though no one knows exactly where—is imaginable enough. But one may wonder at its military prepotence. Why is this pan-Islamic army so much mightier than the pan-Islamic army that has kept trying and failing to defeat the army of Israel? And what about the armies of, say, Europe, India, Russia, China, and America?

It is a tribute to the power of ideology, of shared illusion, that someone as bright as the author could live for so long at this distance from likelihood. Two events disabused him. One was a killing. "The fucking Christian niggers need to be taught a lesson," argued a colleague, following a dispute at Tower Hamlets College (the dispute was about the use of a pool table); and Husain duly sees the black boy lying in a welter of blood. The second event had to do with a woman, his future wife: "Of the many faces I encountered on a daily basis there was one belonging to a girl called Faye that did what mine used to do a lot: smile. As an Islamist I had lost my ability to smile." Although Husain doesn't make too much of this epiphany, we can imagine the inner rearrangement; hereafter, sexual tension is eased, not by religious rage, but by sexual love.

This was in 1996. During his detox and rehab period, Husain re-embraced the gentle Sufism of his parents and his *pir*. He also did something that may be recommended to all

British Islamists: he spent time in Islamic lands. Not a long weekend in some Waziristani boot camp (where, one gathers, it's car bombs all morning, poisons and acids all afternoon, and maniacal misogyny all evening), but extended stays in Syria and Saudi Arabia. Husain comes to love Damascus, despite the sexism, racism, homophobia, and the heroization of such questionable figures as Hitler and Saddam. But he can do nothing with the "loss, mayhem, perversion and hypocrisy" of Riyadh and Jeddah. His wife is continuously accosted and propositioned with hisses and whispered obscenities. And when they visit the Prophet's tomb—dicing with *shirk* (polytheism, idolatry), which is *haram* (forbidden)—"[we] risk being kicked in the face by the Wahhabi guards if we so much as bow our heads." By now we are used to the idea of sexual tension and religious rage in counterbalance within an individual psyche; in Saudi Arabia, tension and rage are the twin predicates of an entire society.

Ed Husain has written a persuasive and stimulating book. But as he builds to his affirmatory conclusion he visits a false dichotomy on us, and one that has recently gained an undeserved respectability. He wants to be "free from the fanaticism of secularism or religion"; he wants to "oppose hatred of all forms, secular and religious." In this general view, fundamentalists are on one wing, atheists are on the other, and the supposed center is occupied by moderate believers and a few laconic agnostics. Secular fanaticism, secular hatred—these equivalences are fictions. The humanist pit bulls Richard Dawkins and Christopher Hitchens, I am confident, have very few affinities with Ayman al-Zawahiri and Abu Musab al-Zarqawi. The key point, of course, is that secularism contains no warrant for action. One can afford to be crude about this. When Islamists crash passenger planes into buildings, or hack off the heads of hostages, they shout, "God is great!" When secularists do that kind of thing, what do they shout?

MAY 2007. *The Times*

September 11

"In my humble," as one of Updike's Pennsylvanians likes to put it (sparing himself the chore of saying "opinion"), the name for what happened on September 11, 2001, is "September 11." In fact, "September" alone may eventually prove adequate—just as every Russian, ninety years on, knows exactly what is meant by "October." But the naming of September 11, that day, that event, naturally fell to America. And America came up with something pithier: "9/11."

They are inconsistent, over there, on the matter of abbreviation. For example, they would rather say "FWD" than "four-wheel drive," even though the supposed contraction adds two syllables (and let's not forget that worldwide fatuity "www," which cuts three syllables down to nine). On the whole, though, if a phrase is constantly on American lips, then Americans will seek to shorten it. Why knock yourself out saying "Jennifer Lopez" when you can save precious time with "J-Lo"? And if you want to include "Ben Affleck" in your sentence, there is the thrifty "Bennifer," giving a dividend of five syllables (as does the cineast's code for Brad Pitt and Angelina Jolie, "Brangelina").

9/11 is a couple of syllables shorter than September 11, and is to be warmly congratulated on that score. Of course, no one refers to Independence Day as "7/4"—or to Halloween as "10/31" or to Christmas as "12/25"—but such anniversaries are hardly the theme of year-round discussion. Further to recommend it, I suppose, 9/11 sounds snappy and contemporary and wised-up, like "24/7." True, there is the unfortunate resemblance to "911," the national phone number for the emergency services (the equivalent of our 999), but this distraction pales before 9/11's triumphant and undeniable brevity. In addition, though you may have your doubts about its appropriateness, and its utter lack of historical resonance (where is the French Avenue 7/14, the Italian Piazza 4/25?), 9/11 does have the humble merit of unambiguously denoting September 11.

Or at least it does in America. In the U.K., 9/11 can't even manage that. Yes, even this menial task is beyond it. As everyone knows (in another section of their minds), the British system proceeds, rather more logically, from small things to large: day, month, year. So 9/11 doesn't denote September 11—not over here. I have no attachment to our way of doing it, and there's a case for the comprehensive adoption of the American method, if only to economize on our embarrassment. Such a switch would be ridiculous, admittedly, but it would only be ridiculous *once* (rather like our celebration of the millennium, with po-faced pomp, exactly a year too soon); it wouldn't go on being ridiculous forever.

Then came the attacks, in London, of July 7, 2005. And within a matter of hours, it seemed, we were gazing at that truly pitiful contrivance, "7/7" (a nickname, incidentally, that

America has not adopted). Well, at least 7/7 was palindromic, and we could evade the day-month anomaly with which we had saddled ourselves; and perhaps we could go on evading it, so long as Islamism confined its "spectaculars" to such dates as January 1, February 2, March 3, and so on. But the postponement was brief. A fortnight later we learned of the bungled bombings of July 21—and hereafter the consensus silently cracked. In the press it is not uncommon, now, to see references to "the 21/7 trial" on the same page, or even in the same piece, as the usual stuff about 9/11.

I don't really care which way round they go: my principal objection to the numbers is that *they are numbers*. The solecism, that is to say, is not grammatical but moral–esthetic—an offense against decorum; and decorum means "seemliness," which comes from *soemr,* "fitting," and *soema,* "to honor." 9/11, 7/7: who or what decided that particular acts of slaughter, particular whirlwinds of plasma and body parts, in which a random sample of the innocent is killed, maimed, or otherwise crippled in body and mind, deserve a numerical shorthand? Whom does this "honor"? What makes this "fitting"? So far as I am aware, no one has offered the only imaginable rationale: that these numerals, after all, are Arabic.

Meanwhile, in Great Britain, nearly all our politicians, historians, journalists, novelists, scientists, poets, and philosophers, many of them deeply anti-American, have swallowed the blithe and lifeless Americanism, and go on doggedly and goonishly referring to September 11 as November 9. Why? For the LCD reason: everyone does it because everyone does it; it is the equivalent of a verbal high five. But the cunning of history, the cunning of Clio, that satirical muse, has already made a firm reckoning. September 11, 2001, is the most momentous event in world history since the end of the Cold War. And the Cold War ended when the Anti-Fascist Protection Barrier, otherwise known as the Berlin Wall, was decisively breached—on November 9, 1989. That is to say, on 9/11.

The above, I suggest, is a very minor parable about the herd instinct: the herd instinct and its tolerance of nonsense. The rolling creed we call Islamism is also an embrace of illusion, as indeed is religion itself—a massive and multiform rearguard action, so to speak, against the fact of human mortality. Our own performance, in what we may limply but accurately call the struggle against those who use terror, has also shown signs of mass somnambulism and self-hypnosis. This is true at the executive level, insofar as the Iraq misadventure (and much else) is a corollary of the neoconservative "dogma"; and it is true on the level of individual response. Six years later, we are all still learning how to think and feel about September 11.

In the summer of 2006 I came back to live in the U.K. after two and a half years in South America. I maintain that I had not become more of a fascist in the interim—at the feet of a Galtieri, say, or at the knee of a Pinochet. But in politics it is surprisingly easy to move from side to side while staying in the same place; and the middle ground, I discovered, was not where it used to be. The extent of the shift became dramatically clear to me on live television, when I appeared on *Question Time* (the BBC's interactive discussion show) and was asked about our progress in what was now being called the Long War.

The answer I gave was, I thought, almost tediously centrist. I said that the West should have spent the last five years in the construction of a democratic and pluralistic model in Afghanistan, while in the meantime merely containing Iraq. In Afghanistan we have already seen, not the "genocide" eagerly predicted by Noam Chomsky and others, but "genogenesis" (in Paul Berman's coinage)—a burgeoning census. Since 2001, the population has increased by 25 percent. Meanwhile, too, needless to say, the Coalition should have been tearing up the earth of Waziristan in its hunt for the remnants of al-Qaeda.

At this point I started looking from face to face in the audience, and what I saw were the gapes and frowns, not of disagreement, but of disbelief. Then a young woman spoke up, in a voice near-tearful with passionate self-righteousness, saying that it was the Americans who had armed the Islamists in Afghanistan, and that therefore the U.S., in its response to September 11, "should be dropping bombs on *themselves*!" I had time to imagine the F-16s yowling in over Chicago, and the USS *Abraham Lincoln* pumping shells the size of Volkswagens into downtown Miami—in bold atonement for the World Trade Center, for the Pentagon, for United 93, United 175, American 11, and American 77. But then my thoughts were scattered by the sound of unanimous *applause*.

We are drowsily accustomed, by now, to the fetishization of "balance," the ground rule of "moral equivalence" in all conflicts between West and East, the 100 percent and 360-degree inability to pass judgment on any ethnicity other than our own (except in the case of Israel). And yet the hand-clappers of *Question Time* had moved beyond the old formula of pious paralysis. This was not equivalence; this was hemispherical abjection. Accordingly, given the choice between George Bush and Osama bin Laden, the liberal relativist, it seems, is obliged to plump for the Saudi, thus becoming the appeaser of an armed doctrine with the following tenets: it is racist, mysogynist, homophobic, totalitarian, inquisitional, imperialist, and genocidal.

As I drafted this piece (in early July 2007), Dr. Kafeel Ahmed—the furious, steaming, orange-hued hulk we saw applying himself at Glasgow Airport—lay slowly and expensively dying in the burns unit of the Royal Infirmary. At that time, too, we were learning about the men who planned and botched the attacks of July 21, 2005. And certain questions could now be asked in a rather less self-reproachful spirit. It might even be that we have ceased to toady to those who proclaimedly seek our murder.

Was Ladies' Night at the Tiger Tiger discotheque a legitimate target for Dr. Ahmed's "anger" about Iraq? Were the morose North Africans of July 21 "desperate" about Palestine? And what do all the U.K. jihadis have in common, these brain surgeons and jailbirds, these keen cricketers and footballers, these sex offenders, community workers, ex-boozers and drug addicts, primary-school teachers, sneak thieves, and fast-food restaurateurs, with their six-liter plastic tubs of hairdressing bleach and nail-polish remover, their crystalline triacetone triperoxide and chapatti flour, and their "dockyard confetti" (bolts and nuts and nails)? And the answer to that question seems to be slowly dawning. What they have in common is this: they are all abnormally interested in violence and death.

Let us briefly trundle through the argument for moral equivalence, and let us begin with a trio of ascertainable truths. First, the years 1947 and 1948 saw two imperialistic decisions that guaranteed an increase in hostility between Muslim and non-Muslim: the partition of India along religious lines, and the establishment of the state of Israel. (These decisions also led to, but did not invent, murderous hostility between Muslim and Muslim—in East Pakistan, in Gaza.) Second, throughout the 1970s the Arab regimes sponsored by the U.S. started to head off political dissent by guiding the opposition toward Islamic fundamentalism. And, third, in the 1980s the U.S. backed the mujahidin against the Soviet Union in Afghanistan, and also helped fund the Pakistani madrasas, whose graduates (all of them unemployable zealots) increased from 30,000 in 1987 to well over half a million by 2001.

Thereafter, or so the equivalence argument goes, the Islamist vanguard, having wearied of seeing the battles fought exclusively on their own soil, visited a taste of this destruction on the West. Which turns out to suit the neocons and Christian Zionists, who can now place the U.S. under military rule while they prepare their push for Islamic oil and for Israeli hegemony in the Middle East. The goals of the so-called "terrorists" (who are merely responding in kind to state terrorism from the U.S. and its clients) are not delusive or messianic but solemnly political. So it has always been: the oppressed struggle against the oppressor; the wrongs of the past rise up to avenge themselves on the present.

The equivalence line always anticipates the usual counterargument, which it considers to be an orientalist smear: that the Islamists are fanatics and nihilists who, in their mad quest for world domination, have created a cult of death. With each passing day, however, the counter-argument is sounding like an increasingly sober description of reality. With the twentieth century so fresh in our mind, you might think that human beings would be quick to identify an organized passion for carnage. But we aren't quick to do that—of course we aren't; we are impeded by a combination of naïveté, decency, and a kind of recurrent incredulity. The death cult always benefits, initially at least, from its capacity to astonish and stupefy.

Gathering what we can from the works of such thinkers as Sayyid Qutb, Abul Ala Mawdudi, and Abu Bakr Naji (the author of *The Management of Savagery*), and from various pronouncements, fatwas, ultimatums, death threats, and suicide notes, we may compare radical Islam with the thanatoid political movements we know most about, namely Bolshevism and Nazism (to each of which Islamism is indebted). Of the many affinities that emerge, we may list, to begin with, some secondary characteristics. The exaltation of a godlike leader; the demand, not just for submission to the cause, but for utter transformation in its name; a self-pitying romanticism; a hatred of liberal society, individualism, and affluent inertia (or *Komfortismus*); an obsession with sacrifice and martyrdom; a morbid adolescent rebelliousness combined with a childish love of destruction; "agonism," or the acceptance of permanent and unappeasable contention; the use and invocation of the very new and the very old; a mania for purification; and a ferocious anti-Semitism.

But these are incidentals. Thanatism derives its real energy, its fever and its magic, from something far more radical. And here we approach a pathology that may in the end be unassimilable to the non-believing mind. I mean the rejection of reason—the rejection of the sequitur, of cause and effect, of two plus two. Strikingly, in their written works and their table talk, Hitler and Stalin (and Lenin) seldom let the abstract noun "reason" go by without assigning a scornful adjective to it: worthless reason, craven reason, cowardly reason. When those sanguinary yokels, the Taliban, chant their slogan, "Throw reason to the dogs," they are making the same kind of Faustian gamble: crush reason, kill reason, and anything and everything seems possible—the restored Caliphate, for instance, presiding over a planetary empire cleansed of all infidels. To transcend reason is of course to transcend the confines of moral law; it is to enter the illimitable world of insanity and death.

This dual negation is for a while intensely propulsive. It gives the death cult its needed momentum—its escape velocity. On the other hand, for our part, the high value we assign to human life is not a matter of illusion or sentimentality or "hypocrisy"; it is not the "Papist-Quaker babble" derided by Trotsky. "Reason," moreover, is one of our synonyms for realism, and indeed for reality; without it, as Islamism will soon find, the ground turns to mire beneath your feet. Death cults are in the end obedient to their own illogic: what they do is die.

Certain actors in the Middle East, Hassan Nasrallah of Hezbollah, Moqtada al-Sadr of the Mahdi Army, and even Ismael Haniyeh of Hamas (Hamas, whose charter goes so far as to "quote" from *The Protocols of the Elders of Zion*), are within evolutionary distance, you feel, of a political process that concerns itself with practical outcomes. Osama, and his bewilderingly repulsive surrogates, are in the position of the Japanese military in the months before Pearl Harbor. Without supernatural intervention on behalf of our divine emperor, the top brass argued, we can't conceivably *win*. But for a time we can raise merry hell. And that's what they decided to go ahead and do.

September 11 means September 11, 2001—the day the towers came down. It was also the day when something was revealed to us. Do we now know what that was? Much of our analysis, perhaps, has been wholly inapposite, because we keep trying to construe Islamism in terms of the ratiocinative. How does it look when we construe it in terms of the emotions? Familiar emotional states (hurt, hatred, fury, shame, dishonor, and, above all, humiliation), but at unfamiliar intensities—intensities that secular democracy, and the rules of law and civil society, will always tend to neutralize. There is religious passion too, of course, but even the bruited, the roared fanaticism seems unrobust. It may even be that what we are witnessing is not spiritual certainty so much as spiritual insecurity and spiritual doubt.

Islamism has been with us for the lion's share of a century. The Muslim Brotherhood was founded in 1928, and within a decade there was an offshoot in what would soon become Pakistan. But the emotionally shaping event, one is forced to deduce, was the establishment of the Jewish Homeland. In the war fought to bring that about, Israel, occupying 0.6 percent of Arab lands and with a proportional population, defeated the armies of Egypt, Syria, and Transjordan, together with the supplementary forces of Lebanon, Saudi Arabia, and Iraq.

In the other 99.4 percent of Arab lands, this event is known as *al-nakba:* the catastrophe. And that epithet hardly overstates the case. The "godless" Soviet Union, after a comparable reverse, might have fallen into troubled self-scrutiny; but what does it mean for peoples who sincerely believe that an omnipotent deity is minutely attentive to their desires and deserts? Having endured several centuries of Christian prosperity, global power and reach, and eventual empire, the Islamic nations were vanquished by a province the size of New Jersey. In the Koran, the Jews are portrayed as cunning and dangerous, yet they are never portrayed as *strong:* "Children of Israel . . . Dread My might." We in the West have ceased to understand the meaning of the word "humiliation," and we use it, in descriptions of our daily struggles, with the lilt of comic hyperbole. Now we must further imagine how it feels to be humiliated, not only by history, but also by God.

This was surely a negative eureka for the Muslim idea. Following the defeat of 1948, and following the defeat (in six days) of 1967, Islam, or its militant vanguard, was finding that it had arrived at a crossroads—or a T-junction. The way to the left was marked "Less Religion," and meant a journey to the future. The way to the right was marked "More Religion (Islam is the Solution)," and meant a journey to the past. Which direction would lead to the return of God's favor? On their left, a stretch of oily macadam, perhaps resembling one of the unlovelier sections of the London orbital, scattered with windblown trash, and, of course, choked and throttled with traffic. On their right, something like a garden path at the Alhambra, cleaner, simpler, and—thanks to the holy warriors and their "smiting of necks"—much, much emptier. In *Al-Qaeda and What It Means to Be Modern,* John Gray reminds us that Islamism, in both its techniques and its pathologies, is on the crest of the contemporary. But the emotions all point the other way; they speak of retrogression and revanchism; they speak of a vehement and desperate nostalgia.

Sayyid Qutb, like someone relaying a commonplace or even a tautology, often said that it is in the nature of Islam to dominate. Where, though, are its tools and its instruments? The only thing Islamism can dominate, for now, is the evening news. But that is not nothing, in a world of pandemic suggestibility, munition glut, and our numerous Walter Mittys of mass murder. September 11 entrained a moral crash, planetwide; it also loosened the ground between reality and delirium. So when we speak of it, let's call it by its proper name; let's not suggest that our experience of that event, that development, has been frictionlessly absorbed and filed away. It has not. September 11 continues, it goes on, with all its mystery, its instability, and its terrible dynamism.

SEPTEMBER 11, 2007. *The Times*

Name Index

Abdalla, Khalid, 133
Abdullah, King, of Saudi Arabia,
 173
Ahmadinejad, Mahmoud, 82,
 123–4, 126, 128
Ahmed, Kafeel, 198
Allawi, Iyad, 82
Amis, Kingsley, 15
Arnold, Matthew, 16
al-Askari, Hasan, 124
Atatürk, Kemal, 187
Atta, Muhammad, 50, 74, 93–121,
 130, 133, 144
Austen, Jane, 17

Bagehot, Walter, 50
Baldwin, Stanley, 166
Bandar, Prince of Saudi Arabia,
 150
al-Banna, Hasan, 58, 62
Barak, Ehud, 68
Bellow, Saul, 8
Berg, Nick, 156
Berman, Paul, 197

Terror and Liberalism, ix, 60,
 67–9, 75
bin al-Shibh, Ramzi, 102
bin Laden, Osama, 9, 13, 74, 80,
 140, 198, 201–2
 as architect of September 11, 4,
 22, 133
 depiction on T-shirts, 47–9
 empowerment of, 142–4
 influenced by Sayyid Qutb, 73
 lack of intelligence, 141–2
 miscalculation of America,
 71–2
Blair, Hazel, 170
Blair, Tony, 159–85
 accent, 168
 alcohol consumption, 161
 appearance, 160, 162, 165, 167
 character and personality,
 159–60, 162, 164–6, 179,
 183–4
 GMTV interview, 162, 165
 on Iran, 161
 in Iraq, 170, 179–85

Blair, Tony (*cont.*)
    and Iraq War and aftermath,
      27, 81, 82, 160–1, 175,
      177–8, 183
    and the Labour Party, 163–4
    his legacy, 162, 163, 168–70
    and his mother, 170–1
    in Northern Ireland, 168–70
    on power, 184
    relationship with Bush, 27,
      81, 160, 167, 172–3, 175,
      176
    religious beliefs, 13, 167, 171,
      179
    on Scottish separatism, 161–2
    and September 11, 160
    staff and bodyguards, 174
    style of governance, 166–7
    in Washington, 172–6
Bottrall, Ronald, 17
Brown, Gordon, 164, 171
Bush, George Herbert Walker,
    147–8
Bush, George W., 8, 147–51
    "axis of evil" speech, 22–3
    and Blair, 27, 81, 160, 167,
      172–3, 175, 176
    character and personality, 81,
      83, 147–9, 175
    hatred of, 83, 198
    and Iraq War, 27–8, 81–4, 139,
      148–50
    loathing of Kim Jong-Il, 23
    profanity erased, 174
    religious beliefs, 13, 23–6, 82
    and September 11, 5, 103, 133
    staff and bodyguards, 174
Bush, Laura, 133, 148

Callaghan, James, 168
Campbell, Alastair, 163, 171
Card, Andy, 148
Carter, Jimmy, 173
Chamberlain, Neville, 166
Cheney, Dick, 148, 172
Cheney, Liz, 84, 88
Chernyshevsky, Nikolai: *What Is
    to Be Done?,* 63
Chirac, Jacques, 27
Churchill, Winston, 84, 166, 173
Clancy, Tom, 4
Clinton, Bill, 55, 147, 173
Conrad, Joseph, 17
    The Secret Agent, 169
    The Shadow-Line, 90–1
Cyrus the Great, 125

Dawkins, Richard, 191
DeLillo, Don, 7
Dickens, Charles: *Hard Times,* 17

Eden, Anthony, 166
Eliot, George, 17
Eliot, T. S., 17
Elizabeth II, Queen, 84
Empson, William, 17

Frye, Northrop, 16

al-Gaddafi, Colonel Muammar,
    155
Geldof, Bob, 167
Gore, Al, 147
Gorky, Maxim, 11, 167
Gray, John: *Al-Qaeda and What It
    Means to Be Modern,* 204
Greengrass, Paul, *United 93*

directed by (reviewed),
129–35

al-Hadjadj ibn Yusuf, 29
Hain, Peter, 169
Halliday, Jon: *Mao: The Unknown Story,* 86
Haniyeh, Ismael, 201–2
Hanjour, Hani, 99, 113
Harris, Sam: *The End of Faith: Religion, Terror, and the Future of Reason,* 70–1, 73, 79, 82
Heath, Edward, 140, 166
Hitchens, Christopher, 61, 191
Hitler, Adolf, 68, 78, 80, 191
  Mein Kampf, 137, 201
Hobsbawm, Eric, 75–6, 78, 123
Hopkins, Gerard Manley, 17
Hulagu (Mongol warlord), 61
Husain, Ed: *The Islamist* (reviewed), 187–92
Hussein, Saddam, 26–7, 29, 83, 191
  doubles, 31–46
  role in September 11, 137
  secularism, 25
  and weapons of mass destruction, 24, 26–9, 80
  Western support for, 126–7

James, Henry, 17
Jarrah, Ziad, 99–103, 104, 132–4
Joyce, James: *Ulysses,* 19
Jung Chang and Halliday, Jon: *Mao: The Unknown Story,* 86

Kafka, Franz: "Josephine the Singer . . . ," 12

Kant, Immanuel, 15
Kazzar, Nadhim, 26
Kemal, Mustafa (Atatürk), 187
Kennedy, Edward M., 169
Kerry, John, 147
Khomeini, Ayatollah, 61, 77, 79, 125–6
Kim Jong-Il, 23
Kinnock, Neil, 173
Krekar, Mullah, 155

Larkin, Philip
  "An Arundel Tomb," 131
  "Aubade," 89
  "Church Going," 90
Law, Andrew Bonar, 166
Lawrence, D. H., 17
Leavis, F. R., 16–17
Lenin, Vladimir I., 11, 63, 126, 184, 201
Lewinsky, Monica, 55
Lewis, Bernard, 59, 82
  The Crisis of Islam, 61
  What Went Wrong?, 78, 87
Lifton, Robert Jay, 79
Lincoln, Abraham, 165
Lindh, John Walker, 71
Livingstone, Ken (Mayor of London), 72, 76
Lloyd George, David, 166

Mahdi, the, 124
Mailer, Norman, 51, 76
Malia, Martin, 9
al-Maliki, Nouri, 180
Mawdudi, Abul Ala, 188, 200
McGinnis, Ken, 176
McGuinness, Martin, 169

Menenez, Jean Charles de, 70
Merkel, Angela, 161, 166–7
Miller, Frank, 151
Mirren, Helen, 184
Muhammad (the Prophet), 49–50,
    88, 107, 124, 188
    tomb, 191
Muhammad, Khaled Sheikh, 96,
    102, 108–9, 140
Myatt, David, 156
Myers, L. H., 17

Nafisi, Azar: *Reading Lolita in
    Tehran,* 63
Naipaul, V. S., 25
    *Beyond Belief: Islamic Excursions
    Among the Converted Peoples,*
    65
    "Tell Me Who to Kill," 9
Naji, Abu Bakr: *The Management
    of Savagery,* 200
Nasr, Vali: *The Shia Revival,* 151
Nasrallah, Hassan, 201–2
Nasser, Gamal Abdel, 57, 125,
    140

Omar, Mullah Mohammed, 54,
    143
al-Omari, Abdulaziz, 93, 94,
    101–4, 106, 110, 115, 116
O'Neill, John, 144

Paisley, Ian, 169
Petraeus, General David, 181
Pol Pot, 80
Porter, Peter: "Once Bitten,
    Twice Bitten," 56
Powell, Colin, 150

Prescott, John, 163
Prophet, the, *see* Muhammad

Qutb, Sayyid, 56–63, 83, 140, 142
    as "father of Islamism," 62–3,
    73, 140, 200, 204
    In the Shade of the Koran, 57–8
    Milestones, 57

Rafsanjani, Akbar Hashemi,
    126
Reagan, Ronald, 13, 23, 25,
    123–4
Reza Pahlavi, Mohammed,
    125
Reza Shah, 125
Rice, Condoleezza, 147–8, 150,
    172
Richards, I. A., 17
Roberts, J. M.: *Twentieth Century,*
    86
Rochester, John Wilmot, 2nd Earl
    of: "Satyr Against
    Mankind," 11
Rove, Karl, 27, 173
Rumsfeld, Donald, 27, 50–2, 81,
    148, 150
Ruthven, Malise: *A Fury for God,*
    79

Sadat, Anwar, 57
al-Sadr, Moqtada, 170, 201–2
Saheb, Fultholy, 188
Saramago, José, 69
Scowcroft, Brent, 147
Senguen, Aysel, 111–2, 132–3
Sharon, Ariel, 68
Sheen, Michael, 184

al-Shehhi, Marwan, 99, 113, 130

al-Shehri, Wail and Waleed, 115, 116

Stalin, Joseph, 78, 157, 201

Steyn, Mark: *America Alone: The End of the World as We Know It* (reviewed), 153–7

Straw, Jack, 177

al-Suqami, Satam, 115, 116

Tafazoli, Jahangir, 125

Talabani, Jalal, 180

Tanweer, Shehzad, 74

Tocqueville, Alexis de, 18

Tuchman, Barbara: *The March of Folly*, 82

Updike, John, 51, 193

Wilson, Harold, 166

Woodward, Bob, 23
Bush at War, 149–50
Plan of Attack, 52, 149–50
State of Denial: Bush at War, Part III (reviewed), 147–51

Wright, Lawrence: *The Looming Tower: Al-Qaeda and the Road to 9/11* (reviewed), 137–45

Yeats, William Butler, 17, 73

Yevtushenko, Yevgeny, 15

al-Zarqawi, Abu Musab, 170

al-Zawahiri, Ayman, 140–3

A NOTE ON THE TYPE

This book was set in a version of the well-known Monotype face Bembo. This letter was cut for the celebrated Venetian printer Aldus Manutius by Francesco Griffo, and first used in Pietro Cardinal Bembo's *De Aetna* of 1495.

The companion italic is an adaptation of the chancery script type designed by the calligrapher and printer Lodovico degli Arrighi.

Composed by Creative Graphics, Allentown, Pennsylvania
Printed and bound by R. R. Donnelley,
Harrisonburg, Virginia
Designed by Peter A. Andersen